P9-CNG-802

Figure improvement
and
Body conditioning
through
Exercise

PRENTICE-HALL INTERNATIONAL, INC., *London*
PRENTICE-HALL OF AUSTRALIA, PTY., LTD., *Sydney*
PRENTICE-HALL OF CANADA, LTD., *Toronto*
PRENTICE-HALL FRANCE, S.A.R.L., *Paris*
PRENTICE-HALL OF INDIA (PRIVATE) LTD., *New Delhi*
PRENTICE-HALL OF JAPAN, INC., *Tokyo*
PRENTICE-HALL DE MEXICO, S.A., *Mexico City*

Figure Improvement

AND

Body conditioning

THROUGH

Exercise

Earl L. Wallis
San Fernando Valley State College

Gene A. Logan
Southwest Missouri State College

PRENTICE-HALL, INC., Englewood Cliffs, New Jersey

ACKNOWLEDGMENT

The authors gratefully acknowledge the assistance of Claudia Hood, an expert in movement and dance, with whom we consulted in designing the continuity exercises. Dr. Roger K. Burke, as a kinesiologist, assisted in our interpretation of the muscles principally involved in some movements.

Although many people have made helpful suggestions that we deeply appreciate, the pages that follow—the emphases, presentations, interpretations, and errors—are the responsibility of the authors alone.

TABLE OF CONTENTS

Figure improvement
and
Body conditioning
through
Exercise

1

THE SCIENTIFIC BASES
FOR FITNESS AND FORM

The human body is remarkably adaptable. Within limits, it has the ability to adapt itself gradually, yet rather rapidly, to accommodate stresses imposed upon it. This progressive adaptation to the stress of muscular work results in an increased ability to perform subsequent muscular activity. However, such adaptation is reversible: the less one does, the less one is capable of doing. Yet, barring disease, with the resumption of exercise, the body may adapt to imposed stresses and improve its capacity to function, regardless of the duration of inactivity.

The body responds rather specifically to demands placed upon it. This concept is advanced as a unifying principle that applies to any of the characteristics that comprise physical fitness. The concept shall be called the SAID principle. This coined word represents the first letters in the following statement: "Specific Adaptation to Imposed Demands." This principle provides a general guide to the design of an exercise program. It has been applied in the design of the six series of exercises contained in this book. The application of the SAID principle leads to a most effective and efficient application of exercise. Using this principle as a guide, it is possible to achieve the maximum effect with minimum effort and time.

This principle is justified in theory and supported by research and careful observation. To obtain results from an exercise program the demands must be sufficient to force adaptation. It is hypothesized that much, if not all, of the adaptation is basically neurological. To illustrate this principle, we will describe some of the involvements in the development of muscular strength or tone.

Skeletal muscles, which move the bones of the body, are composed of thousands of individual muscle fibers, bound together in bundles by connective tissue. The total number of muscle fibers, fixed by heredity, cannot be altered. In a poorly conditioned person many fibers are "latent." That is, they are in an inactive reserve condition but can be reactivated through training.

Muscle fibers contract when stimulated by nervous impulses and relax when the impulses cease. The motor neurons, which stimulate the muscle fibers to contract, travel from the spinal column to junctions with the muscle fibers. Each motor neuron may have as many as a hundred or more branches connecting with individual muscle fibers. A single neuron, together with the fibers it controls, is known as a *motor* unit.

Figure 1. A motor unit is a single motor neuron and the muscle fibers that it controls.

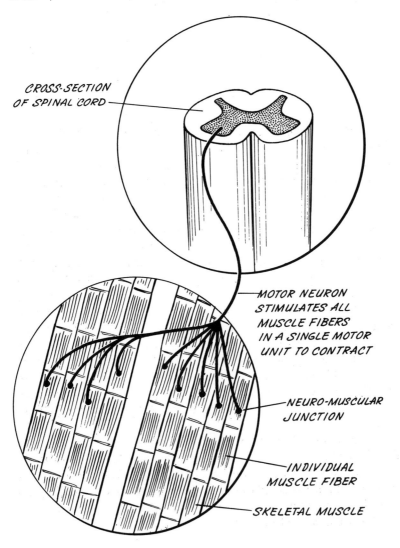

CROSS-SECTION OF SPINAL CORD

MOTOR NEURON STIMULATES ALL MUSCLE FIBERS IN A SINGLE MOTOR UNIT TO CONTRACT

NEURO-MUSCULAR JUNCTION

INDIVIDUAL MUSCLE FIBER

SKELETAL MUSCLE

Many motor units make up a single skeletal muscle. All of the motor units do not function at the same time. The number functioning depends upon the amount of force required to accomplish the task. Greater exertions of force require many motor units; conversely, less intense force requires fewer motor units. The variable rate at which the individual motor units function also determines the force of muscular contraction.

Distributed throughout the muscles are *muscle spindles* and other specialized structures. These generate sensory nervous signals, indicating continuously the length and tension in the muscles. These signals are transmitted to the central nervous system. The muscle spindles are composed of specialized muscle fibers and neurons. In shortening, the contractile muscle fibers of the spindles do not exert

Figure 2. *The muscle spindle. It has other neural functions that are not of concern here. The structures involved in these functions are not shown.*

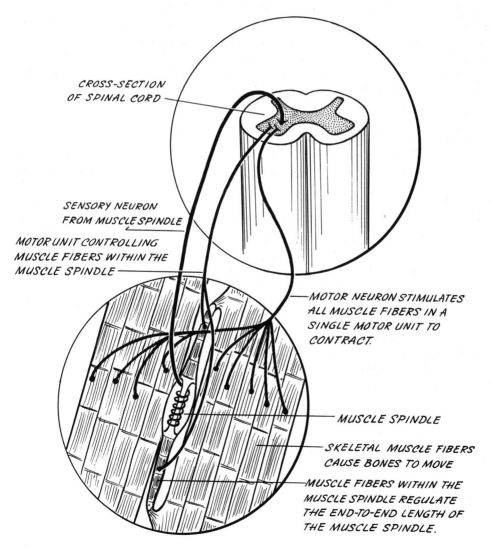

CROSS-SECTION OF SPINAL CORD

SENSORY NEURON FROM MUSCLE SPINDLE

MOTOR UNIT CONTROLLING MUSCLE FIBERS WITHIN THE MUSCLE SPINDLE

MOTOR NEURON STIMULATES ALL MUSCLE FIBERS IN A SINGLE MOTOR UNIT TO CONTRACT.

MUSCLE SPINDLE

SKELETAL MUSCLE FIBERS CAUSE BONES TO MOVE

MUSCLE FIBERS WITHIN THE MUSCLE SPINDLE REGULATE THE END-TO-END LENGTH OF THE MUSCLE SPINDLE.

force on the tendon as do the surrounding skeletal muscle fibers. The function of the fibers within the spindle is merely to regulate the length of the spindle.

The sense organs located in muscles, tendons, and joints that provide awareness of bodily position are known as *proprioceptors*. Muscle spindles are proprioceptors that are vital in the control of movement. Muscle spindles lie parallel to the muscle fibers which contract to move the joints. When the total muscle is stretched or put under tension the spindle is stretched. Elongation of the center portion of the muscle spindle increases the frequency of the nervous impulses discharged by these sensitive organs. The impulses travel to the central nervous system and may further excite the motor neurons which activate the skeletal muscle fibers surrounding the spindle.

In addition to increasing muscular force by heightening the output of the motor neurons, the impulses also serve to regulate the contraction of the few muscle fibers found inside each end of the spindle. The contraction or relaxation of these fibers inside the spindle regulates the tension on the central, stretch-sensitive portion of the spindle. In this way, through "feed-back," the spindle may regulate its end-to-end length and continually be in position to sense tension and to stimulate additional contraction of the surrounding muscle if more force is required to perform the task. The muscle is, in effect, "thinking" for itself. Because the spindle length may be regulated by contraction of its own muscle fibers, it continues to be suitably adjusted so that any change in the muscle length will cause it to discharge impulses.

The operation of these nerve-muscle relationships has application to the development of strength, endurance, flexibility, and skill. If, during a period of progressive conditioning, the nervous system is continually forced, by tension in the muscle, to respond with heightened muscle spindle activity, the skeletal muscle is "trained" to exert more force because the neural function begins to operate with more facility. The impulses flow more freely than before. This phenomenon is known as *neural facilitation*. Since the muscle spindle is a proprioceptor, the facilitation of its function is known as *proprioceptive facilitation*. This is a neurological basis for explaining the SAID principle. Continuing to use strength as an example, it may be seen that increased ability of the muscle to exert force is dependent upon imposing demands that will result in proprioceptive facilitation.

It might, therefore, be said that the body *learns* to be strong through practice in working the muscles against resistance. And the "learning" is rather specific. One may "learn" to use muscles strongly in certain ways and in certain coordinations, but he may find other tasks utilizing the same musculature to be more difficult than would be anticipated.

It should be understood that, in addition to neurological factors, the broader physiological "base" for muscular strength is also elevated through training. That is, the ability to withstand fatigue and generate force is dependent upon adequate oxygen supply and nutritional elements stored within and made available to the contractile tissue. This internal chemical condition and the training of "latent" fibers are involved in improving functional ability. This improved chemical-nutritional foundation can be made to function more efficiently through heightened levels of neural stimulation.

The development of endurance involves a similar neurological basis. Some types of localized endurances result from the continued facilitation of the same mechanisms already described. In addition, endurance involves the elevation of the general base: greater output of the heart muscle, the opening of more capillaries, improved oxygen-carrying capacity of the blood, and other related training effects which are basic adaptations.

An increase in the range of motion of the joints of the body also has a basis in neurological function. Flexibility results from stretching the membranes that surround muscles, stretching tendons, and lengthening the ligaments and other tissues that limit the movement of the joint.

As the muscle on one side of a joint shortens, the muscle on the other side lengthens. To stretch an area there must be a relaxation of the muscles in the area. Without this relaxation the muscle tends to resist the stretching action. As the muscles on one side of the joint are contracted, the muscles on the other side are reciprocally inhibited. Therefore, contracting the muscles opposite the area being stretched provides the favorable conditions for lengthening the connective tissue that surrounds the muscle.

When attempting to increase flexibility through stretching, reflex muscle contraction tends, as a self-protecting mechanism, to limit the range of motion. To

Figure 3. *Basis for endurance. Performance capacity varies with specific "practice" and general "training."*

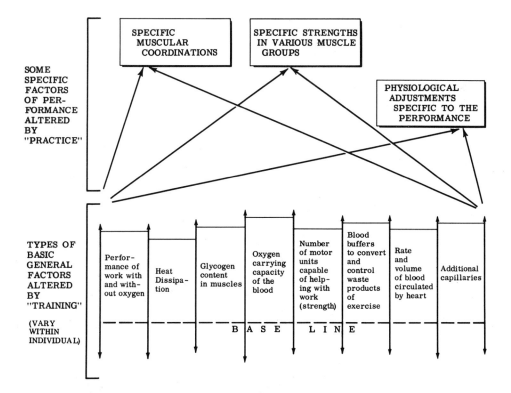

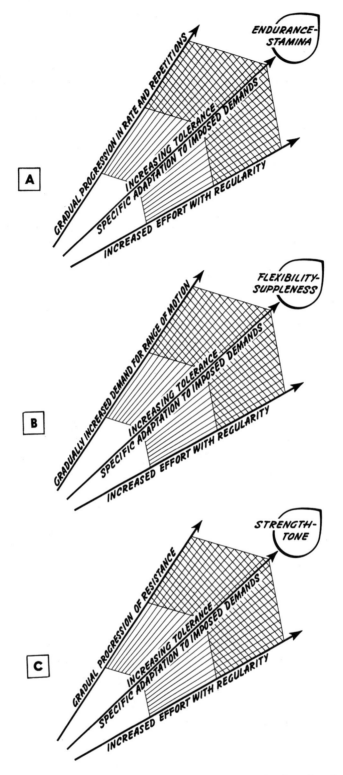

Figure 4. *The elements of fitness and form are developed and maintained as a result of* Specific Adaptations to Imposed Demands.

minimize this reflex activity in the area being stretched, slow, sustained contractions of the muscles opposite are preferable to rapid movements involving momentum. The reflex effort that is required to stop momentum sets the stage for possible muscular injury.

It becomes obvious, then, that the demands placed upon an organism by exercise must be sufficient to force adaptation. Therefore, exercise that is too mild is nearly valueless and is a waste of time.

As mentioned previously there is one major principle, SAID, through which improvement of fitness, bodily function, and form may be achieved. This involves placing the body under stresses of varying intensity and duration. From attempting to overcome these stresses the body adapts rather specifically to these imposed demands and, as a result, elevates the tolerance for further activity of greater intensity. Since individual tolerance for exercise varies, it becomes necessary to have gradation or progression in the intensity or severity of the exercise. This principle of pushing the systems to force their development of endurance, flexibility, and strength underlies the program of exercise outlined in this book.

In Figure 4A the lower arrow represents regularly increased effort. A gradual progression of rate and repetitions is represented by the upper arrow. The middle arrow leading to endurance and stamina indicates the increased tolerance that is an outcome of the combination of regular effort and resistance. The individual's tolerance for endurance activity may be represented by any point along the middle line. This adaptation is made as a result of performing activities that must be sustained over a period of time.

Figure 4B indicates the means of developing flexibility or suppleness. Here it is shown that regularly increased effort, represented by the lower arrow, when combined with activities that involve a gradually increased demand for range of mobility, results in greater joint range of motion.

Figure 4C shows the means for developing strength or tone. With additional effort to gradually increase the resistance against which the muscles can work, there is a specific adaptation to the demands imposed which results in increased tolerance.

The physical fitness elements—strength, endurance, and flexibility—are biological bodily adjustments which are developed gradually according to the stresses applied. These adjustments are also reversible: as a result of disuse the individual becomes less strong, less flexible, and has less endurance. The axiom that form tends to follow function applies to the human body.

Exercise, if sufficiently intense, increases the capacity to perform more exercise. It is the only activity which provides the means to better fitness and form—it is the only way to prevent muscle sag. Without exercise, muscles become lax and flabby, no longer holding the body in shape. It is unquestionably substantiated that one of the values of exercise is the general firming, shaping, and contouring of the muscles. Form follows fitness.

Continuing demands must be placed upon the body in order that these elements of fitness be maintained. Maintenance actually results from small applications or small dosages of stress. This prevents the reversal of the state of fitness which results from disuse of the body.

The condition of the bodily systems and the ability to use these systems allow some people to function better than others. Both this condition and ability can limit fitness and form—both depend upon activity for development. Selected purposeful activity improves fitness and form; inefficient activity or inactivity decreases proper bodily functioning. This book describes some basic elements of fitness and specifically recommends pertinent exercises, activities, and approaches for the attainment of fitness and form.

Obviously these series of exercises are not the only ways in which to cause exercise adaptation. Other types of exercise, as well as sport activities, may be used. However, many sports do not sufficiently place demands on all bodily areas, and some are not sufficiently vigorous. To insure all-around development or maintenance, it often becomes important to use exercise as a supplement to recreational sport activity. The exercises outlined in this book could, however, provide a complete conditioning program.

Without sound information, people too often become fair game for questionable fitness programs, "systems" of body building, body contouring, and weight control. There is an alarming increase in the number of claims made for apparatus and systems that place emphasis upon passive exercise, that is, exercise in which a machine or electric current causes the body to move. All such appeals and practices are not without value, but many are misleading, deceptive, and expensive.

A well-informed person should know what he can do for himself to achieve the outcomes he desires without personal harm or unnecessary expense. To meet his immediate and remote requirements he should understand what properly selected and executed exercises can do.

Noteworthy improvements can be achieved in rather short periods of time; but expectations should be tempered with realism. The following suggestions are listed as curbs for enthusiasm as well as pleas for caution and intelligence. When attempting to increase efficiency through exercise, it is well to remember that:

1. Results are relatively impermanent. Continuous, regularly scheduled activity is essential to the maintenance of fitness once it is achieved.
2. Interest in exercise is difficult to maintain for many people. With others, ·doing exercises often spurs them on. Performing exercise which is exhilarating or stimulating will help to maintain interest.
3. A *variety* of exercises and sports activities should be learned and performed. Narrowness of outlook may result if one type of activity precludes participation in others.
4. Harmful "self-centeredness" may result from too much "self-body-admiration." Too much introspection hinders all-around development.
5. Sustained pursuit of original goals is preferable to a constant shift in objectives.

2

THE MOVEMENT
OF THE BODY

Man must be in sufficient physical condition to resist, adequately, the pull of gravity to maintain an erect posture, without any other demands for body movement. A great deal of his energy is spent throughout the day in combating the force of gravity through the use of muscles that tend to keep him upright. In other words, man is in constant search of body extension. Those muscles which maintain extension may be referred to as the anti-gravity muscles. Constant activity in these muscles can cause man to reach the end of the day in a fatigued state. If these anti-gravity muscles are not in condition, they are not equipped to withstand for many hours the stresses imposed upon them by gravity.

In certain areas of the body, as in the lower back, dense connective tissue known as fascia has a function of reinforcement of active muscle contraction. This holding action of connective tissue "spells off" the anti-gravity muscles of the back and serves as an energy-conserving mechanism. When the anti-gravity muscles tire and their burden is borne completely by the heavy connective tissue of the back, this fascia or connective tissue then becomes adapted to the stress of bearing the weight. A body position that is sustained, as in an increased lower back curve, often results in the shortening of these tissues. Once this adaptive shortening has occurred, the need for flexibility or increased range of motion becomes evident. Often associated with this lack of flexibility is pain, which may result from irritated nerve endings upon movement. This condition occurs not only in the lower back region but in other parts of the body as well.

9

Diagram 1 of Figure 5 illustrates the bones of the skeleton. Theoretically, the bones can be balanced one on another to simulate the upright skeleton. To hold them in this anti-gravity position, we must have muscles at a minimum number of places. Note that the downward pressure of gravity applied to the bones of the skeleton tends to cause it to buckle at three principal points: at the ankle, knee, and hip. Since the weight of the body is largely in front of the spinal column, the body tends to fall forward. In order to counteract these tendencies toward buckling, a minimum of five muscles or muscle groups are involved. Figure 5, Diagram 2, shows these muscles and their relationship to the upright skeleton. If muscle 4, the back muscle, shortened if would pull the trunk backward. Therefore, muscle group 5, the abdominals, is required to hold the rib cage and pelvis together. The abdominals, therefore, function as "reflex," anti-gravity muscles. Exercises for these anti-gravity muscles are fundamental to any general conditioning exercise program.

Some tissues, although not contractile, serve an anti-gravity function. This applies to the lumbar fascia, neck, and other parts of the body as well. Any faulty postural situation in which the body is habitually held erect by fascia and not solely by muscle may result in this adaptive shortening. Because of the adaptive shortening that takes place as a result of the continual use or overuse of the flexor apparatus, the "sitting man" has a great concern for flexibility. Compensation must be made for weakened muscles or faulty alignment in order for the body to be held upright against gravity. The shortened fascia and connective tissues take over the function of the weakened muscles. Thus the function of fascia may become over-efficient. If the fascia adapts to a shortened position the muscles on the opposite side of the joint may not be allowed to shorten completely when they contract. This prevents action through a full range of motion. In order to have a full range of motion, flexibility exercises are required. In other words, lack of flexibility is an adaptation to the disuse of the muscles on the opposite side of a joint. A principal concern, therefore, is for the areas that have adaptively-shortened connective tissue due to weakened muscles on the opposite side. Even though high levels of strength and endurance have been attained, optimum flexibility is required in order that the segments of the body be properly aligned and balanced.

A well-rounded program of exercise necessitates the development of flexibility or suppleness together with strength and endurance. There is an interrelationship between flexibility, strength, and endurance which is a prerequisite to proper body alignment.

In order to clarify muscle-bone relationships, an understanding of the points made in Figure 6 is important before proceeding with a description of specific exercises. Diagram 1 simply indicates that bony levers come together to form joints. The joints shown in the diagram are those of the elbow and shoulder, which are held together by ligaments. Diagram 2 shows how muscles typically cross the joints and are in a position to apply tension and move the bones. It will be noticed that the muscles terminate in tendons which are attached to the bones. All things being equal, a muscle pulls with the same tension from both ends. If the muscle pulled from both ends, the shoulder blade would move upward at the shoulder joint and the forearm would move upward at the elbow, as illustrated in Diagram 3. There-fore, if the forearm is to be moved at the elbow joint it is necessary to stabilize the shoulder joint. This stabilizing or fixing mechanism indicated by the "X" is pic-

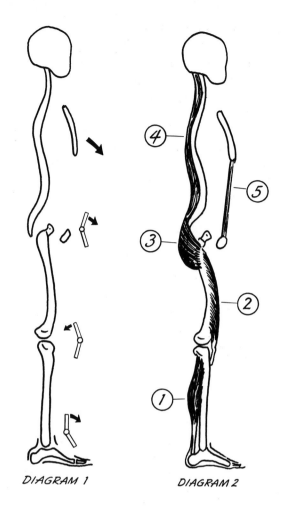

Figure 5.

DIAGRAM 1   DIAGRAM 2

Figure 6.

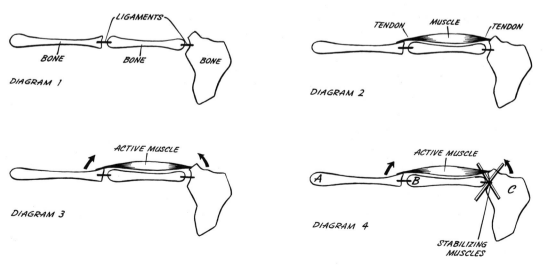

LIGAMENTS

BONE   BONE   BONE

DIAGRAM 1

TENDON   MUSCLE   TENDON

DIAGRAM 2

ACTIVE MUSCLE

DIAGRAM 3

ACTIVE MUSCLE

A   B   C

DIAGRAM 4

STABILIZING
MUSCLES

11

tured in Diagram 4. In the development and consideration of an exercise one must be concerned with the stabilizers as well as with the muscles that produce the action. In designing the exercises shown and described in this book this principle has been taken into account because any exercise for a specific part of the body involves muscles of other parts as well.

Too often, people are of the belief that the benefits of exercise are limited or nonexistent. Actually, a great deal is known about the values and benefits of exercise which has not been adequately communicated. It is not the purpose of this book to provide an exhaustive substantiation of the values for which there is now ample scientific evidence. It is only through muscular activity that benefits accrue. Muscular activity provides for the maintenance, improvement, and development of various systems of the body. The bony framework of the body must support the weight of all of the other systems against the pull of gravity. It receives much of its stimulus for growth and development from the tensions which result from muscles pulling on their bony attachments. There is ample evidence that without sufficient muscular activity growth is impaired.

As the muscles pull on the bones to perform movements, a demand is placed on other systems of the body. This is of particular importance, for the demands made on other systems to supply fuel for energy require them to adapt to stresses.

Of singular importance in efficient functioning is the cardio-vascular system. This includes the blood-vascular system, lungs, and heart. It is the increased demands placed upon this system by the muscular system that causes blood to be forced into the tissues. In responding to these demands, fitness of this system is developed. It should be realized that, as a muscle works, the blood-vascular system within it is being exercised. The response of blood vessels to this demand of muscular activity is the only way that the blood vessels can be exercised. The use of exercise to maintain tone of the cardio-vascular system is of extreme importance in view of the increasingly high incidence of cardio-vascular disorders. This is of particular concern in later life. Current medical opinion indicates that cardio-vascular disturbances may be delayed or prevented through judicious use of exercise.

The pumping action of the heart distributes blood to the various parts of the body. The return of blood to the heart allowing for recirculation during activity is principally dependent upon the squeezing action of muscles on the veins. Veins have valves within them which allow the blood to go in one direction only. A major benefit of exercise is the development of strength and tone in the muscles that assist in pumping the blood back to the heart.

The involuntary or smooth muscles—for example, the ring-like bits of muscle found in the arteries—need exercise as well as do the voluntary or skeletal muscles of the body. This exercise can be accomplished only by placing demands on this muscle, which results only from stressing the cardio-vascular system.

It must be remembered that the heart itself is a muscle which responds to exercise. Only by placing demand on this muscle is it possible to increase its functional capacity. This really means that the heart becomes capable of satisfying the demands for blood imposed by the other systems of the body upon the cardio-vascular system. Because of improvement in functional capacity resulting from exercise, the greater the demand for blood in the tissues of the body, the greater becomes the capacity of the heart to meet that demand.

In reviewing the values of exercise it becomes evident that it is the muscular system and the demands upon it that pull along the development of fitness of all the other systems of the body.

Not to be underemphasized as a value of exercise is the improvement of form and appearance of the body. The development of strength and tone, endurance and stamina, and flexibility and suppleness is related not only to improved function but also to improved appearance and form. Among the outcomes of attempting to achieve the factors enumerated above are improved contouring and hypertrophy (or bulk) of the muscle which may be important from a cosmetic standpoint. In addition, through exercise the body has a remarkable facility to develop symmetry. That is to say, developing one side of the body through exercise results in a closely corresponding development of the other side. Improving the strength-tone of skin muscles is another important cosmetic aspect of exercise.

No precise claim can be made showing that exercise is linked with length of life. However, it cannot be denied that exercise aids in the retention of functional ability. One of the functional capacities commonly lost by older people is range of motion, or flexibility-suppleness. There is no doubt that in most instances this shortening of muscle and connective tissues result from inactivity in earlier life.

Another commonly observed effect of aging is atrophy or wasting away of tissue due to inactivity. The fact that muscles sag and lack tone in inactive middle-aged and older people is too commonplace to need elaboration here. The only prevention for this atrophy or wasting away is to engage in those activities that are designed to develop and maintain strength and tone.

Another common problem among older people, as mentioned before, is the increasing prevalence of circulatory disturbances. According to medical opinion, many of these problems arise as a result of inactivity. Again, exercise is the only solution.

A strong case has been made for the values of exercise, but it could not be claimed that fitness and form can be developed with exercise alone. For example, there is a close relationship between diet and exercise. This relationship involves a simple balance between caloric intake and energy output when weight control is considered. But a general state of adequate nutrition is required for the maintenance and development of body tissues.

Other benefits of activity exist although not as clearly understood or substantiated as those previously discussed. These values relate to how one "feels." The person who regularly participates in activity is well aware of the pleasant, exhilarating feeling that results from vigorous exercise. The vitality of the individual is heightened not only by the enjoyment of participation in activity but also by a subsequent pleasant feeling. It is following activity that the relaxing benefits of exercise are realized. The relaxation that follows physical activity is a major justification for activity. This is "natural" relaxation. Activity which aids relaxation in this way probably provides a form of emotional release from the tensions of daily living as well.

3

MISCONCEPTIONS
ABOUT EXERCISE

In spite of abundant evidence concerning the effect and benefits of exercise, there is an astonishing number of misconceptions about its function and use. For example, the idea persists that concentrating on the development of fitness among children will result in subsequent adult fitness. The fitness of children is important because it influences and stimulates growth and development, but it must be realized that in order to retain fitness during adult years, exercise must be employed at appropriate levels and durations commensurate with the individual's tolerance through his life span. In other words, the maintenance of physical fitness is an ongoing, persistent necessity that may not be solved by the conditioning of children alone.

Another popular misconception is that people live longer if they participate regularly in exercise. Evidence to support this claim is sparse. This does not mean, however, that the functional capacity is not sufficiently improved and maintained in order to justify regular participation in suitable exercise.

Claims have been made in favor of time-consuming systems of exercise that place insufficient demands upon the body. These systems are categorized as calisthenics or "arm-waving" exercises. Criticism of calisthenics lies mainly in the inefficient use of time, resulting from an inadequate imposition of stress in proportion to the amount of time spent. In other words, exercise should be commensurate with the tolerance capacity of the individual. The application of stresses that would raise the tolerance capacity of the individual, would more judiciously utilize time. Some of the exercises described in this book may appear to be calisthenic, but these have been selected for the individual with a low tolerance capacity. This exercise involves an imposition of a high demand upon this individual in relation to his capacity to perform.

Claims are made asserting the permanent and lasting effects of exercise. Most of the effects of exercise are not permanent. The adjustments made by the body to stress or imposed demands are largely reversible: without continuing demands, capacity diminishes. The benefits of exercise tend to be fleeting: they cannot be retained unless regular activity is maintained.

The misconception continues to persist that deep breathing is a fundamental exercise. It is difficult to conceive the advantages of such an exercise. A critical analysis of this exercise reveals that the blood is not further oxygenated by forced inspiration, that lung capacity is not greatly increased, and that resistance to respiratory diseases is not developed. On the basis of present knowledge, time spent on such exercise is not justified. Any intentional regulation of breathing rate and rhythm is unnecessary since the breathing apparatus is reflexly, or automatically, regulated by the demands imposed upon it.

There is also the notion that the way in which one breathes during exercise has some influence upon strength development and other fitness factors. There is no substantiation for this belief. Exercise is usually best performed without any conscious attention to breathing. The one exception applies when a maximum effort is made against resistance. When maximum effort is being exerted, the trachea (wind-pipe) which should be kept open as a safety measure to prevent possible harmful effects caused by extreme intra-abdominal and intra-thoracic pressures. These pressures might cause weakened blood vessels to rupture or other types of herniations. During extreme efforts, breathing helps to prevent these possible harmful effects and to prevent the build-up of pressure. Specific breathing exercise may be prescribed for therapeutic purposes, but for those participating in normal conditioning programs, breathing exercises are of little consequence.

Another misconception concerning the function of exercise is that it improves general coordination. Exercise does not specifically facilitate the performance of a skill if coordination is used in terms of the general motor ability to perform skilled acts. However, improvement in strength, endurance, and flexibility may provide the basic essentials upon which skill may be built. In other words, the development of strength, endurance, and flexibility through exercise does not enable the individual to better perform specific coordinations. However, a minimum level of these factors, which can be developed through exercise, is essential as a foundation for the development of specific coordination.

4

EXERCISE
AND WEIGHT CONTROL

In an inactive, sedentary society overweight is a great health problem. Although weight control is not a problem for everyone, it concerns a major portion of the adult population. To those beset with overweight or underweight difficulties, control of weight is a time, energy, and too often, a money consuming problem. Although weight control theories and practices are relatively simple there is an alarming amount of confusion. Millions of dollars are spent annually on weight-reduction nostrums and schemes advertised as "easy, quick, pleasant and permanent." The abundance of remedies is rivaled only by the number of unsatisfied participants. Sound knowledge, used correctly, is the best method of controlling body weight.

Overweight may be due to emotional stress, disease, a glandular condition, overeating, and lack of exercise. The diet is most frequently involved, and treatment is usually successful when dietary corrections are made. It is important to follow the advice of a medical advisor because weight fluctuations may indicate serious disease or glandular conditions. Especially important is the rate and manner in which a person reduces his weight.

The most effective weight-reduction procedure must involve the use of exercise, the role of which is often misunderstood in weight control. Two erroneous ideas persist: that appetite increases proportionately to an increase in physical activity thus nullifying any weight-reduction achieved through the activity; and that an immense amount of work or exercise is required for a very small loss in weight. It must be remembered that weight can be altered by changing the caloric *intake and consumption.* In the absence of glandular defects, a person will usually gain weight when the caloric intake exceeds the number of calories expended by activity. Some people, however, are exceptions to this rule. These individuals, although their caloric intake may far exceed the requirements for their activity level, do not store the excess as fat. When caloric intake is not sufficient to support the energy needs of the body, the individual will lose weight.

In other words, there are two ways of losing weight: either increase energy expenditures through activity or reduce caloric intake by diet. Actually, a combination of the two is best. It is true that strenuous exercise or work can enable one to lose weight, but this is true only if there is no increase in caloric intake. By reducing the caloric intake the body is forced to use up the fat stored in various depositories. Body weight can be reduced by burning about four thousand calories per approximate pound. If the daily diet is restricted by five hundred calories per day or the daily *activity is increased* by five hundred calories per day, a pound can be lost in eight days. It is evident that the effects of exercise are cumulative. One could see the dramatic, achievable results in the course of a year if this approach were continually applied.

Rolling machines, motor-driven bicycles, vibrators, and other devices intended to assist in weight reduction, as well as massage, pinching, and electrical stimulation are based upon the theory that fatty tissues disintegrate thus resulting in loss of weight in the selected area or spot on the body. Facts show that the possibility of "spot" reducing is very questionable. When one reduces, he loses fat deposits all over the body. Claims that flabby thighs can be slimmed or that double chins can be removed by massage should be viewed with considerable suspicion.

In the deposit of fat associated with overweight, it has been observed that a weight-reduction program first influences those areas in which the fat was last deposited. In other words, weight can be expected to be lost in those areas in which it was last gained. It has also been observed that fat deposits vary in distribution from person to person: a similar exercise-diet program will not achieve similar results for everyone.

For these reasons, an apparent "spot reducing," or localized loss of weight, is possible due to diet and exercise. It is not established, however, that exercise can shift and relocate fat. Nonetheless, an area from which fat has been taken may be recontoured through the development of muscle strength and tone in that area.

One of the most frustration-producing misconceptions is that exercise can drastically alter certain hereditary, bodily configurations. This is, of course, not possible. Development must take place within the restriction of initial hereditary endowment: physical potential is predetermined by hereditary factors. Exercise can do wonders but it is not a panacea. Overenthusiasts, who view exercise as a cure-all, set unattainable goals and expectations. The value and judicious use of exercise should be viewed in proper perspective.

The limitation of caloric intake is of particular significance with advancing age because of metabolic changes which may alter the dietary requirements. The same caloric intake for the young adult and for the middle-aged person of the same proportions, if sufficient to maintain normal weight for the young adult, usually results in a weight gain for the middle-aged person. This is due not only to differences in activity and caloric requirements but also to a general modification in metabolic rate. The older person requires a lower caloric intake to maintain his body at rest. If this middle-aged person maintains the appetite of the younger person, the appetite he had at age twenty, it is then reasonable that he will continue to gain weight. Results of exercise and dieting are only permanent as long as these aspects of living are given consideration and practice.

5

THE USES
OF EXERCISE

People obviously vary in their ability to perform given amounts of exercise. The suitability of exercises suggested in this book depends upon the individual's tolerance for exercise. This tolerance is best determined by progressing gradually through the sequences of exercises outlined. This procedure will enable the individual to determine his fitness and tolerance. The exercises are designed to progressively increase demand as the tolerance of the individual for exercise is elevated.

Many physical fitness tests have been devised in an attempt to appraise the fitness level of individuals. The utility of these tests may be questionable. There are at least two reasons for this lack of confidence in such tests: first, different fitness tests, when applied to the same individual, yield varying results; second, physical fitness test scores, established through evaluating large numbers of people, do not necessarily apply to all individuals. It has often been observed that subjective evaluation of an individual's state of fitness is more valid and meaningful than scores from a standardized test.

If the individual gradually discovers his own tolerance for exercise, the possibility of strain and overdoing in the early stages is minimized. To summarize, no physical fitness test is necessary since the fitness of the individual is determined by his ability to do the exercises. The person expediently adapts himself to the program at the appropriate level commensurate with his tolerance to perform.

For the individual who has not engaged in vigorous activity for a long period of time, more exploration will be required to determine the

19

tolerance level. For the person of low tolerance the possibility of muscle soreness should be considered. A rule of thumb is that if soreness persists past the second day following the workout, the exercise has probably been too strenuous. If muscle soreness persists for a longer period at any level of tolerance, the demands imposed have probably been too great.

At this point the question arises, "How frequently should a person exercise?" It might be said that once a week is not often enough, that every day is not necessary, and that three times a week is about right. The question also arises, "How vigorous should each session of exercise be?" This is a highly individualized matter, but for the person who is beginning an exercise program enough activity to induce slight tiredness is adequate.

Still another question frequently arising concerns the progression or intensification of exercise. The best means of increasing the intensity of imposed demands is described in the sections dealing with each of the series of exercises.

This book provides a systematic approach to conditioning through exercise. Some elements of conditioning and values of exercise have been described but the major portion of this book is concerned with the presentation of six series of exercises. Each series has been designed to produce specific outcomes. The particular values of each are discussed in detail in the introduction to the presentation of each series. There is, however, a relationship among the various series of exercises. In most cases they will be used to supplement each other. The series of exercises are (1) Endurance; (2) Flexibility; (3) Isometric Conditioning; (4) Isotonic Conditioning; (5) Figure Improvement; and (6) Continuity Exercises.

First in the series is Endurance Exercises. This series is intended not only for the development of endurance and stamina, but also for warm-up procedures which precede and supplement the other series of exercises. Warm-up implies an increase in circulation and a subsequent improvement in the pliability of tissues. The activities recommended for warm-up, if sustained at a rapid rate, are those that develop cardio-vascular endurance. It is recommended that activities of the type suggested in this series precede flexibility exercises.

Series Two, the Flexibility Exercises, is designed to maintain or improve the range of motion of the joints. The use of this series is essential.

Series Three, Isometric Conditioning Exercises, involves the development of strength and tone by exerting effort without movement. This type of exercise may efficiently develop strength in a minimum period of time: only a few minutes per exercise period are required. However, it is important that isometric exercise be supplemented by endurance and flexibility exercises to provide a well rounded program.

Series Four, the Isotonic Conditioning Exercises, provides a program for the gain or maintenance of strength and endurance. This series of exercises is probably not as efficient in the development of strength in relation to the time spent; but the stimulation of circulation, the development of endurance, and the improvement of strength justify the use of these exercises.

Series Five, Figure Improvement Exercises, concentrates on particular exercise problems of women. The principal concern for this series of exercises is to improve appearance. Not only are these exercises intended to improve form but also to improve and maintain fitness.

Series Six, the Continuity Exercises, is also intended primarily for women. This series was designed to develop stamina, suppleness, and tone in an interesting sequence of movements. Consideration was made for the problem areas of the body. The continuity series of exercises is a total conditioning program in itself. This rhythmical approach to conditioning exercise provides interest and has a wide application.

Although the general reader may be interested only in the exercises recommended, the reader interested in more detail may find the kinesiological analysis of muscles involved in each exercise to be of value. This information is separate; an understanding of these details is not essential to comprehend the exercises described.

Although adults are demonstrating the exercises, they apply to children, youth, and older adults as well. Wise selection of exercises is based upon the tolerance of the individual to perform. The fact that some exercises seem to be more appropriate for women than for men, or vice versa, does not preclude any of the exercises being used by either sex of any age. Finally, it must be remembered that in keeping with the SAID principle, exercise facilitates the performance of more exercise and only by these means do fitness and form result.

6

THE DEVELOPMENT
OF ENDURANCE

The aspect of fitness that seems of greatest value to most people is that of endurance or stamina. The ability to make a rapid recovery following a vigorous period of exercise or work is important. The person with developed stamina not only recovers more rapidly but also continues exercise or work longer with less fatigue than a person less fit. To achieve stamina or endurance one has to work specifically for it. The specific demands imposed on the organism, if endurance is to be developed, must place stress upon the cardio-vascular system. That is, stress must be placed on the heart, the blood, and the blood-transport system.

This series has been placed first because it has a dual purpose. These activities are utilized to increase endurance and as warm-up activities not only prior to the other series but also prior to sport activity. If this series is used primarily for the purpose of warm-up, it would not be required that the activity be carried to the same intensity or duration as would be necessary if these exercises were solely used for the development of endurance.

Endurance may be defined as the ability to continue a particular activity for an indeterminate length of time: thus a postponement of fatigue. Various activities, however, may differ markedly from one another, and it is important to understand that there are several different kinds of endurance. For example, one kind of endurance is required for four hours of typing, another for an all-day hike, and a third for running a half-mile race. There are as many kinds of endurance as there are

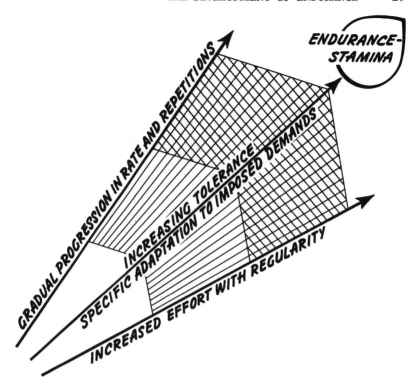

Figure 7. *The development of* endurance-stamina *or the ability to sustain activity—to do more for a longer period with less fatigue.*

kinds of activity; but for practical purposes, the concern here is for cardio-vascular endurance.

When the limit of endurance is reached, people say that they are "out of breath." Actually, cardio-vascular endurance involves two functions: the ability of the breathing apparatus to take in large quantities of oxygen and to give off large quantities of carbon dioxide, plus the ability of the heart and blood circulatory system to transport these substances to and from the muscles. Cardio-vascular endurance therefore depends upon the ability of the heart to increase its blood output. In order to accomplish this the heart must (a) grow strong through exercise as any other muscle, (b) increase its rate of beating, and (c) increase the amount of blood it can pump at each stroke. Building endurance involves, among other things, strengthening the heart muscle.

The Development and Maintenance of Endurance

1. *Intensification of imposed demands.* To develop endurance, the activity should be of such intensity and duration that "normal" limits are exceeded, and body functions are pushed toward their maximum level. The exercise should result in a greatly elevated rate of breathing, and should not terminate until the individual is temporarily "out-of-breath." Any activity which results in accelerated breathing and pulse rate, will develop endurance if sustained for a sufficient length of time.

Any activity in which the same result occurs may be substituted for these exercises. Several active sports achieve endurance development by the normal course of activity. Rapid walking for 15 minutes would be excellent for most adults in sedentary occupations. Walking does not create a sufficient demand for the development of a higher level of endurance however. Activities such as swimming, bicycling, rowing, hiking, and running are excellent endurance builders.

2. *Duration.* The prolongation of exercise is effective. Thus, if the objective is to develop sufficient endurance to hike or ski all day, a moderate activity such as walking may be employed. The duration of the exercise must be emphasized, for the results of the conditioning will not be satisfactory unless long periods are spent in exercise. This is an application of the SAID principle: adaptations are specifically made to the demands imposed.

3. *Progression.* Both intensity and duration of exercise should be regularly increased in proportionate increments dependent upon the tolerance of the individual. With regular conditioning exercise, endurance is built rapidly. In a week, progress should be noticeable. As endurance increases, it is necessary to employ greater intensity and duration of exercise if further progress is to result. With a stringent program involving intensification, duration, and progression of exercise, a person may reach a high level of endurance in as little as four weeks.

4. *Regularity.* The development of endurance requires frequent exercise sessions at fairly regular intervals. Roughly, three days of activity a week constitute a minimum program. If only three days each week are employed, it is important to space them, for it would be foolish (and ineffective) to exercise for three successive days followed by four days without exercise.

5. *Maintenance.* Once a satisfactory level of endurance has been achieved, this level may be maintained with much less time and effort than was necessary to achieve it. The principle of progression is no longer necessary. Intensification and duration should still be employed, but the exercise will seem much easier and perhaps more pleasant when it is no longer necessary to increase the intensity. But the principle of regularity is still as important as ever. Endurance cannot be stored for future use, except for periods of a few days. As soon as exercise is discontinued, endurance is lost approximately as fast as it was built. Even very short and modified exercise periods could prevent such a loss: it is much easier to maintain endurance than to rebuild it.

The other series of exercises outlined in this book, with the exception of the continuity series, places a rather insufficient demand on the development of endurance. They do, however, contribute to the strength factor which is a prerequisite to endurance training. As recommended, these activities do not sufficiently elevate the respiration and pulse rate to force adaptation. These activities do not demand a greatly heightened supply of oxygen during exercise. Progressive resistance exercise is ideal for developing strength, if resistances that are sufficiently heavy are used. For building endurance, lighter resistances and longer durations are necessary.

The exercises described in this section, although not the only activities that promote the development of endurance, are designed to involve large muscle groups in a total movement activity. All bodily areas are included with this group of exercises.

Endurance-Stamina Exercises

EXERCISE 1

This endurance-stamina exercise involves rapidly repeated jumps on both feet. While in the air the knees should be drawn as high as possible. The exercise should be continued until a state of mild fatigue is experienced.

Kinesiological Analysis:

▲ Factor most developed: Endurance-stamina (warm-up).

▲ Muscle groups most involved: Illustration 1: Ankle, Knee, Hip and Back Extensors. Illustration 2: Knee and Hip Flexors, Abdominals.

EXERCISE 2

This sit-up exercise, repeated rapidly, is designed to develop endurance-stamina. As the arms are thrown toward the feet and the head lifted, the knees should be brought to the chest in one continuous movement. A rapid return should be made to the starting position and the exercise should be repeated until mild fatigue occurs.

Kinesiological Analysis:

▲ Factor most developed: Endurance-stamina (warm-up).

▲ Muscle groups most involved: Shoulder Extensors, Abdominals, Hip and Knee Flexors.

EXERCISE 3

Running in place to develop endurance-stamina should be done with the knees lifted as high as possible. Touching the knees to the hands, which are held level with the elbows, should be attempted with each step.

Kinesiological Analysis:

▲ Factor most developed: Endurance-stamina (warm-up).

▲ Muscle groups most involved: Hip, Knee, and Ankle Flexors and Extensors.

Exercise 4

The two positions of this rhythmic, endurance-stamina exercise are illustrated with the left leg being activated. From the starting position, seen in the first illustration, the left leg is thrust backward and upward as the back is arched. This exercise is then repeated using the other leg.

Kinesiological Analysis:

▲ Factor most developed: Endurance-stamina (warm-up).

▲ Muscle groups most involved: Illustration 1: Hip and Knee Flexors, Abdominals, Neck Flexors. Illustration 2: Hip, Back, and Neck Extensors.

Exercise 5

This endurance-stamina exercise is similar to running in place. It is done by flexing one leg while extending the other in the position shown. The hands do not move. This exercise is not as demanding as others in this group and is recommended for those with rather low endurance tolerance. The exercise should be repeated until a mild state of fatigue is experienced.

Kinesiological Analysis:

▲ Factor most developed: Endurance-stamina (warm-up).

▲ Muscle groups most involved: Flexors and Extensors of Hip, Knee, and Ankle.

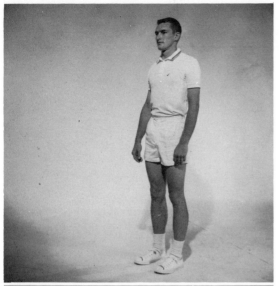

Exercise 6

Three illustrations are shown for this four-count exercise that is designed to promote endurance and stamina. (The fourth position is the same as the second position.) If performed rapidly, this exercise can be very strenuous, therefore it is recommended that it not be done by individuals who have a low tolerance for endurance-stamina activity. The rate should be high enough so that this exercise could not extend for more than a minute.

Kinesiological Analysis:

▲ Factor most developed: Endurance-stamina (warm-up).

▲ Muscle groups most involved: First movement: Extensors of Spine, Hip, Knee, and Ankle. Second movement: Extensors of the Spine, Hip, and Knee. Third movement: Abdominal muscles and Flexors of the Hip and Knee. Fourth movement: Extensors of the Spine, Hip, Knee, and Ankle.

Exercise 7

This endurance-stamina exercise involves rhythmical, free, swinging movements. In this exercise it is particularly important to avoid a complete knee bend in the positions shown in Illustrations 7B and 7D. As the body is lowered to position 7B, the arms swing downward and backward where they remain as the knees are slightly straightened in position 7C. Then, as the arms begin to swing forward, the body is again lowered before swinging up as shown in Illustrations 7E and 7F.

Kinesiological Analysis:

▲ Factor most developed: Endurance-stamina (warm-up).

▲ Muscle groups most involved: Flexors and Extensors of the Shoulders, Extensors of the Spine, Hip, Knee, and Ankle.

7A

7B

7C

7D

7E

7F

7

THE DEVELOPMENT
OF FLEXIBILITY

A reasonable degree of flexibility is required for sufficient bodily movement. In order for the muscles to move the body levers—the muscles opposite those performing the movement must lengthen sufficiently. Ligamentous joint structures and other connective tissue also restrict the range of motion, for inactivity causes these tissues to lose their extensibility. If range of motion does not exist, it can be regained through judiciously applied flexibility exercises.

The sedentary living habits of most people and the habitual use of the flexor apparatus are often major reasons for lack of flexibility. Lacking sufficient activity to stimulate the maintenance of the anti-gravity muscles of the body, "sitting man" habitually uses the flexor muscles, thus developing the requirement for flexibility exercises in certain areas of his body. These areas are generally the posterior thigh, anterior hip, low back, neck, and the pectoral area.

An increase in the flexibility of the body can be accomplished. This is done by stretching the muscular membranes and tendons, and by lengthening the ligaments and other tissues that limit the movement of the joint. The range of movement of body parts is best increased by approaching the limit of stretch slowly and gently, continuing to stretch a little beyond the point of pain. It must be remembered, however, that if residual pain is noted the following day, overstretching has probably occurred.

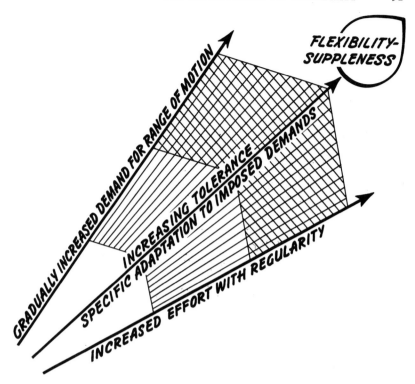

Figure 8. *The development of* flexibility-suppleness *or the range of motion of the joints of the body due to the elasticity and the extensibility of tissues.*

Here again the SAID principle applies. If flexibility is to be developed, the individual must regularly increase effort while gradually increasing the demand for range of motion. Through this activity, specific adaptation to the imposed demand will result. Therefore, the individual may develop tolerance or movement through a greater range of motion. This is shown in Figure 8.

A lessening of flexibility, a reversal of this principle, will result in adaptive shortening of the tissues involved. Poorly conditioned anti-gravity muscles often bring about the commonly seen "fatigue posture." If this posture is sustained for a long period of time, adaptive shortening of some tissue structures occurs. Habitually assuming a properly aligned posture helps to maintain flexibility.

The range of motion through which body parts can be moved is an important factor in daily activity. The ability to bend, twist, and reach is dependent upon the degree of flexibility the individual possesses.

A person can have the muscular system of his body highly developed in terms of strength-tone and still be quite inadequate in physical activity. Though well equipped to handle the problems of strength, one might not be flexible enough to enable him to move easily.

There seems to be some difference in the natural amount of flexibility possessed by various people. Some have shorter muscles, some have shorter ligaments, and some have bodily proportions that cause them to appear less flexible.

Extreme flexibility is of little value in normal activity. The value of being reasonably flexible is the ability to move effectively and to maintain a relaxed, balanced body alignment: to do this, normal joint motion is needed. Joint motion greater than normal may be either of use or a hindrance. This depends upon sufficient strength to support the additional flexibility. For example, increased flexibility in the ankle joint might make it possible for the foot to have a greater range of motion and possibly result in the ability to exert more force in some movements. However, without the proper amount of strength and coordination to bear the weight of the body, the foot can be put in a very weak position. This, of course, can result in injury to the ankle. Less than normal flexibility, on the other hand, could cause injury as a result of inelasticity—the failure of the body part to "give."

The important thing to remember about flexibility is that a greater range of motion can be developed by progressively stretching muscles, ligaments, and other tissues. This is best accomplished by slowly stretching until there is some discomfort—then stretching a bit further.

In developing flexibility, through the use of the exercises described in this series, it is further recommended that the muscle opposite those being stretched be actively contracted during the exercise. For example, in an exercise in which the back of the thigh is stretched as the person is bending forward, a slow, sustained contraction of the abdominal and other anterior muscles is preferred to rapid, bouncing motions. The slow stretch is recommended as a safeguard against possible injury that might occur if rapid, bouncing, stretching motions are made. Another safeguard against injury during flexibility exercises is the need for warm-up activities: the exercises suggested in the Endurance Series should precede the use of the flexibility exercises.

Flexibility-Suppleness

STRETCH 1

This hamstring stretch (Billig) is designed to increase the range of flexion in the lower back and at the hip joint. The arms are placed in the indicated position merely for convenience and balance. The left leg is held as straight as possible, as the right leg is placed in front of it. As one bends slowly from the waist while simultaneously contracting the abdominal muscles, the right elbow is projected diagonally downward about five times. This exercise should be repeated to the opposite side.

Kinesiological Analysis:

▲ Area most involved: Lumbar Spine, Posterior Hip and Thigh.

STRETCH 2

The purpose of this exercise is to increase the range of flexion in the lower back and at the hip joints. This movement may be performed while sitting or standing: in each case the flexed hip and knee position is assumed first. Then an attempt is made to straighten the legs while the original position of the arms is maintained. The abdominal muscles should be strongly contracted as the legs are straightened.

Kinesiological Analysis:

▲ Area most involved: Lumbar Spine, Posterior Hip and Thigh.

STRETCH 3

These lower back stretching exercises, done either sitting on a chair or the floor, involve pulling the body forward and downward with a strong contraction of the abdominal muscles. Stretching this area is made more effective with the knees bent since the muscles of the back of the thigh do not limit the movement.

Kinesiological Analysis:

▲ Area most involved: Lumbar Spine.

STRETCH 4

This stretch is primarily designed to increase the range of flexion of the upper spine. The hands should be pressed downward against the floor and the abdominal muscles should be strongly contracted to facilitate the stretch.

Kinesiological Analysis:

▲ Area most involved: Thoracic and Cervical Spine.

STRETCH 5

This spinal rotation stretch may be done either standing or sitting. The sitting exercise shows the beginning position and the performance of the stretch. Pulling, with the hands against the thigh, provides additional force for this rotation stretch. In the standing exercise an attempt is made to look over the shoulder at the heel of the opposite foot.

Kinesiological Analysis:

▲ Area most involved: Cervical, Thoracic, and Lumbar Spine.

Stretch 6

This stretch, done in a cross-legged, "tailor-sit" position, involves pressing downward on the knees to increase the flexibility of the inner thigh structures.

Kinesiological Analysis:

▲ Area most involved: Adductors of the thigh.

Stretch 7

This stretch is designed to increase flexibility in the chest area. This allows the shoulders to be held back and in a balanced position. With the arms stabilized and held straight on a chair, the head and chest are pulled downward by strong contractions of the abdominal muscles.

Kinesiological Analysis:

▲ Area most involved: Pectoralis Major, Pectoralis Minor, Serratus Anterior.

Stretch 8

Standing the length of the upper arm from a wall, the forearm is placed against the wall at shoulder level. The heel of the other hand is placed in the area just behind the hip joint. With the legs kept straight and the abdominal and gluteal muscles strongly contracted, the pelvis is pressed diagonally forward and to the opposite side.

Kinesiological Analysis:

▲ Area most involved: Pelvic region.

THE DEVELOPMENT OF
STRENGTH OR TONE

Of all components of physical fitness, the factor of strength is undoubtedly the most basic. Muscle development tends to "pull along with it" the development of other factors of fitness. General vitality depends upon the condition of the large muscles of the trunk, especially the abdominal and the back extensor muscles. Weakness of muscles limits the potential achievement in other factors such as posture, endurance, and the performance of physical activities.

Each person inherits a certain number of muscle cells or muscle fibers, and this number cannot be increased. As strength is developed, the thickness, or cross sectional areas and functional ability of the existing fibers are increased. It is true that some people inherit more fibers than others; they have a greater maximum strength potential for this and other reasons.

Muscle size and muscle strength are related: it is true that there may not be a corresponding increase in muscle size proportionate to an increase in muscle strength. The one thing a muscle can do is to develop tension within itself, thus the tendency to pull its two ends together. It cannot push those ends apart. Therefore, muscles or groups of muscles tend to be arranged in pairs on opposite sides of joints. One member of the pair is capable of bending the joint; the other, of straightening it. The members of the pair are said to be antagonistic. They perform opposite functions, providing that no outside forces enter the situation. For example, the biceps muscle on the front of the arm is able to bend the elbow joint. The triceps muscle on the back of the arm is able to straighten the elbow joint.

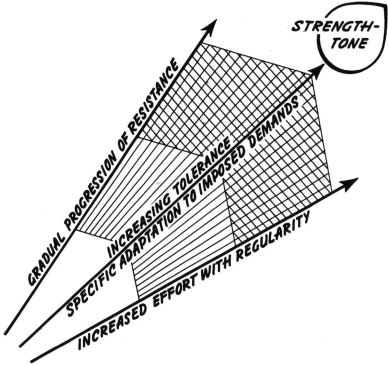

Figure 9. *The development of* strength-tone *or the ability to exert force against resistance—strength.*

Under certain circumstances, however, there is an interesting modification of this concept of antagonistic action. Gravity, an outside force, may enter and modify the situation so that the arm can be first bent and then straightened while the biceps is tense and the triceps is relatively relaxed. Imagine a ten pound weight held in the hand. If the biceps develops exactly ten pounds of effective tension, the weight may be held stationary. This is called *isometric* contraction. Although effort is being made and muscle tension is developed, the length of the biceps remains unchanged. Next, if the biceps develops additional tension it will shift, and the weight will be lifted as the elbow is bent. This is called *concentric* or shortening contraction. Now suppose the tension in the biceps is reduced to less than ten pounds of effective tension. The force of gravity would overcome the tension in the biceps, and the arm would be straightened. In this case, gravity is responsible for moving the arm; the biceps acts as a brake to prevent the elbow from snapping painfully out of control as a result of the straightening position. As the elbow straightens the biceps will be lengthening, although it is still technically considered to be "contracted." Lengthening contraction is called *eccentric* contraction. In both concentric and eccentric contractions the body levers are moving. This is known as *isotonic* contraction. A strength development program may involve increasing demand either isometrically or isotonically.

Although there has been more concern and investigation surrounding the problem of strength development than any other factor of conditioning, there are alarming numbers of misconceptions. One of the commonly believed fallacies is that additional strength impairs speed or coordination: that this does not occur has been proven scientifically.

Another misconception is that muscular strength itself is able to cause "muscle-boundness" or lack of flexibility. A muscle is a collection of bundles of small contractile muscle fibers surrounded by noncontractile connective tissues. Strength is related to the function of the contractile tissues, while flexibility or suppleness and lack of flexibility or "muscle-boundness" are related to the noncontractile connective tissues. Therefore "muscle-bound" is an ambiguous term; if it does exist, it refers to flexibility and not to strength. This matter is discussed more fully in the section on flexibility.

Contrary to some beliefs, there is no food that has special influence on the development of strength, provided that a normal, balanced diet is provided. It is true that the protein requirements of the body are somewhat greater during periods of growth or rapid strength development: high protein diets are not necessary if the phrase "high protein" is interpreted to mean more protein than is ordinarily recommended in a basic diet for an active person. In addition, fluid intake has little or nothing to do with the development of muscle. In summary, there is no way of developing strength without contracting the muscle.

9

ISOMETRIC CONDITIONING EXERCISES

Great improvement in strength in a short time can be achieved through an isometric conditioning program. Isometric exercise involves the production of tension in motionless muscles for brief periods of time. These "no-movement" exercises develop strength with a minimum investment of time, while producing maximum development. Though only minimum time is invested, this exercise produces gains in strength that are equivalent to programs far more time-consuming.

Although an optimum program for strength development, this does not sufficiently stimulate the cardio-vascular system in order to force the development of endurance. For this reason it becomes important to include activity which develops endurance-stamina together with exercises recommended in the isometric conditioning series.

Supplemented by rapid walking, bicycling, hiking, rope skipping, or other activity that stimulates the cardio-vascular system, the use of isometric exercise is an ideal method for maintaining minimum levels of fitness for daily living, with the investment of a minimum amount of time. In other words, there is no more *efficient* way to cause heightened level of strength tone than isometric exercise.

The strong recommendation for this type of exercise is that scientific findings have demonstrated the efficiency of this program in developing strength. For example, in one day, no more strength can be gained by means other than one, maximum contraction, sustained for approximately ten counts, with each exercise. Experiments, in which repeated contractions have been used to the point of exhaustion, showed no further gain than could be attained through one maximum contraction held for approximately ten seconds. As astonishing as this appears, investigators have substantiated these findings.

Because of the simplicity of this kind of exercise, it was possible, in designing the exercises recommended in this series, to suggest various ways that isometric exercise might be done. Three groups of exercises are outlined that might be used according to the existing facilities. The first group involves nothing more than a doorway and the floor. The second group utilizes a door expansion bar. The third group applies to school programs or other programs in which exercise is done in an open area and in which another person is available to provide resistance. These three groups of exercises do not progress from one to the next: each group is designed for the same purpose. They are different ways of accomplishing the same end.

Isometric exercise is a valuable *supplement* to other exercises or sports programs because of its simplicity and rapid results. Other exercises may not place sufficient demands on all parts of the body for development and maintenance. In school situations isometric exercise has a particular application. Often, too little time is available for the developmental aspects of the program: isometric exercise provides a rapid and convenient way to obtain strength tone. Simple isometric exercise is easily taught in the school program: it might consequently be used as a "home" program for youth and adults as well.

Another distinct advantage of isometric exercise is that it is a safe program: a person is the judge of his own capacities. Other types of resistance exercise involve overcoming a definite amount of resistance whereas isometric exercise allows the individual a maximum contraction while functioning within his own limitations. In other exercises, when resistance may be greater than can safely be overcome, muscular strain or joint injury may result if proper precautions are not taken.

The body may be accidentally placed in disadvantageous positions during movement or isotonic exercise. While attempting to recover from an awkward position, injury may result to muscles unable to respond to demands placed upon them. This caution need not be taken with isometric exercise because there is no movement.

The principle of progression, involved in all developmental programs, can be applied to isometric exercise. This is a result of the ability to increasingly exert higher levels of tension to force adaptation. This again, is an application of the SAID principle. Adaptations are made to the specific demands imposed upon the organism. In the isometric exercises it is possible to increase the demands as more strength is developed. As the ability to exert more force is developed, power is progressively elevated.

Isometric Conditioning

Isometric conditioning exercises are divided into three groups. The first group is a general isometric exercise program useful to both sexes of all ages, involving no special equipment. The second group, designed mainly for men and boys, is another all-around program utilizing a door expansion bar. The third group of exercises, that involves one person providing the resistance for another, is designed especially for school and athletic situations where no apparatus is available to provide resistance.

EXERCISE 1

Abdominal strength-tone is basic to any conditioning program. It is sometimes difficult for individuals to understand the feeling of proper pelvic alignment. This feeling, along with the development of strength-tone, results from the following exercise. The first illustration indicates the starting position, a slightly exaggerated low back curve in which the lumbar section of the spine is lifted from the floor. Moving from this position to one in which the lumbar area is forced against the floor, the pelvis is placed in the exercise position. Simultaneously, a strong contraction of the abdominal and gluteal muscles is made. This position should be maintained for ten counts. This exercise not only develops the strength and flexibility that enables the pelvis to be held in a balanced alignment while in an upright position, but also contributes to waist slimness.

Kinesiological Analysis:

▲ Factors most developed: Strength-tone, Flexibility of Lumbar Spine.

▲ Muscles most involved: Rectus Abdominis, External Oblique, Internal Oblique, Transversus Abdominis, Gluteus Maximus.

Exercise 2

The purpose of this exercise is to develop strength-tone of the abdominal muscles in order to promote better posture and to slim the waist. Two means of performing this abdominal exercise are shown. With the feet stabilized under a chair, the trunk is moved to approximately a 45-degree angle. If this position cannot be held for ten counts the trunk should be held more erect. As the ability is developed to maintain this position of less stress, progression should be made to the position illustrated. When the tolerance to perform this exercise increases so that the position may be held for more than ten counts, the arms should be moved to the position behind the head, as illustrated. An effort should be made to flatten the abdominal wall while the position is held. For further intensification of this exercise, a weight may be held behind the head, the size of which depends upon the tolerance of the individual.

Kinesiological Analysis:

▲ Factor most developed: Strength-tone.

▲ Muscles most involved: Rectus Abdominis, External Oblique, Internal Oblique, Transversus Abdominis.

Exercise 3

This exercise involves the strength-tone development of most of the posterior muscles of the body, including the strength-tone development of the back of the upper arm and shoulder. The latter occurs when pressure is exerted downward with the hands. An effort is made to raise the pelvis from the floor while the head, hands, and heels maintain contact with the floor. If the position illustrated is not achieved, attempting to reach the position will progressively increase tolerance until the position can be achieved. This position is held with maximum effort for ten counts.

Kinesiological Analysis:

▲ Factor most developed: Strength-tone.

▲ Muscles most involved: Erector Spinae, Posterior Deltoid, Triceps, Rhomboids, Middle and Lower Trapezius, Gluteus Maximus, Semitendinosus, Semimembranosus, Biceps Femoris, Gastrocnemius.

Exercise 4

The purpose of this exercise is to increase the strength-tone of the flexor muscles at the elbow and the shoulder. The hands are forcibly pressed downward and an attempt is made to flex the elbows. Maximum effort should be sustained for ten counts.

Kinesiological Analysis:

▲ Factor most developed: Strength-tone.

▲ Muscles most involved: Biceps, Brachialis, Coracobrachialis, Anterior Deltoid, Serratus Anterior, Pectoralis Major.

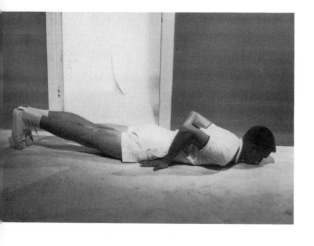

Exercise 5

The purposes of this exercise are to develop strength-tone and to tone the muscles that maintain proper postural alignment of the shoulders. By strengthening the muscles which pull the scapulae together, the shoulders may be held in a balanced position for long periods of time with less fatigue. This exercise also contributes to the strength-tone development of the back of the upper arm. A maximum effort should be made to force the elbows against the floor for ten counts.

Kinesiological Analysis:

▲ Factor most developed: Strength-tone.

▲ Muscles most involved: Rhomboid, Middle Trapezius, Posterior Deltoid, Long Head of Triceps.

Exercise 6

This exercise is designed to strengthen and tone the muscles of the back upper arm. The exercise involves forcing the hands outward from the body against a door jamb. This effort, which is exerted for a maximum of ten counts, employs the muscles which extend the elbow.

Kinesiological Analysis:

▲ Factor most developed: Strength-tone.

▲ Muscles most involved: Triceps.

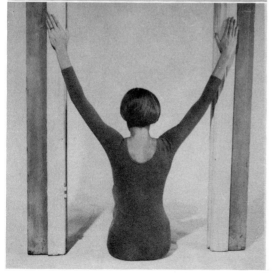

Exercise 7

These three exercise positions are designed to strengthen and tone the muscles of the chest. Although other muscles are involved, the three positions illustrated place specific emphasis on the development of the pectoralis major. The first involves the upper pectoralis major, the second the middle, and the third the lower. The back should be kept in an erect position while each of these positions is held, exerting maximum force, for ten counts.

Kinesiological Analysis:

▲ Factor most developed: Strength-tone.

▲ Muscles most developed: Pectoralis Major, Pectoralis Minor, Serratus Anterior, Coracobrachialis, Anterior Deltoid, Short Head of Biceps.

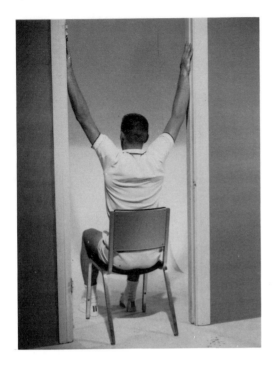

EXERCISE 8

The purpose of this exercise is to develop strength-tone in the muscles of the back of the arm and some muscles of the rib cage. The lower portion of the pectoralis major and the latissimus dorsi muscles are principally involved and are difficult to develop without special apparatus. The hands should be pressed outward against the door jamb while holding the elbows as straight as possible for ten counts.

Kinesiological Analysis:

▲ Factor most developed: Strength-tone.

▲ Muscles most involved: Latissimus Dorsi, Pectoralis Major, Pectoralis Minor, Triceps, Posterior Deltoid, Teres Major, Rhomboids.

EXERCISE 9

This exercise develops the strength-tone of the muscles of the back upper arm as well as those surrounding the shoulder joint. The shoulder joint, vulnerable in most people to injury due to insufficient strength and development, requires more strength to provide protective stability than most other joints. The shoulder is dependent upon muscles to maintain its functional stability more than any other major joint. In this exercise, maximum force should be exerted for ten counts while holding the elbows as straight as possible.

Kinesiological Analysis:

▲ Factor most developed: Strength-tone.

▲ Muscles most involved: Trapezius, Deltoid, Triceps.

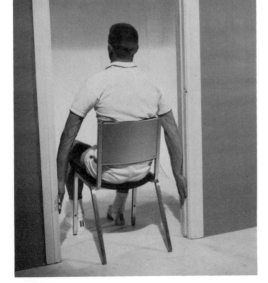

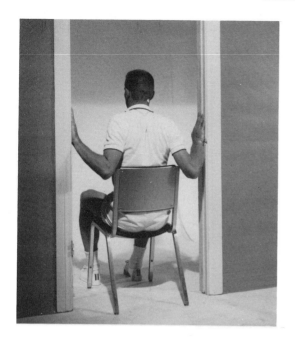

Exercise 10

This exercise is designed to develop the strength-tone of the muscles that straighten the elbow. Maximum pressure should be exerted directly outward for ten counts.

Kinesiological Analysis:

▲ Factor most developed: Strength-tone.

▲ Muscles most involved: Triceps.

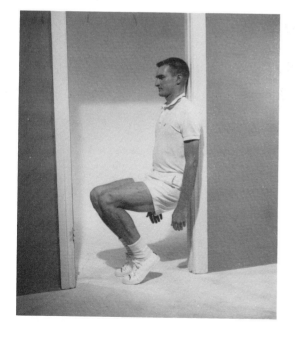

Exercise 11

This exercise strengthens and tones the muscles of the front thigh and calf area. To achieve the exercise position, the person should stand about ten inches from a wall gradually lowering the body to a simulated sitting position. When the thighs are parallel to the floor, the heels should be raised as high as possible. The position is held for ten counts.

Kinesiological Analysis:

▲ Factor most developed: Strength-tone.

▲ Muscles most involved: Rectus Femoris, Vastus Medialis, Vastus Intermedius, Vastus Lateralis, Soleus, Gastrocnemius.

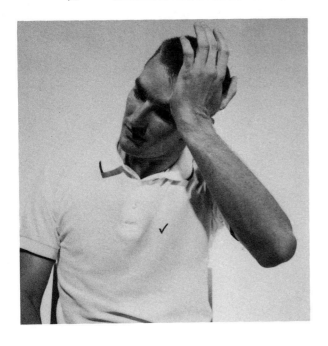

EXERCISE 12

This exercise is designed to develop the strength-tone of the front and side neck muscles that rotate and flex the head. To activate the left flexors and rotators, the face should be turned to the right with the head pressed downward against the resistance offered by the left hand. After holding this position for ten counts, the exercise should be repeated to the opposite side.

Kinesiological Analysis:

▲ Factor most developed: Strength-tone.

▲ Muscles most involved: Sternocleidomastoideus.

EXERCISE 13

The purpose of this exercise is to strengthen the large, skin muscle that covers the area from the base of the jaw to the upper chest. The extent of this large, flat muscle is clearly shown in the illustration. Proper conditioning of this muscle helps to prevent sagging. The exercise is executed by clenching the teeth, raising the head slightly, and forcefully pulling the corners of the mouth outward and downward until tension is felt throughout the entire area. This position should be held for ten counts.

Kinesiological Analysis:

▲ Factor most developed: Strength-tone.

▲ Muscles most involved: Platysma.

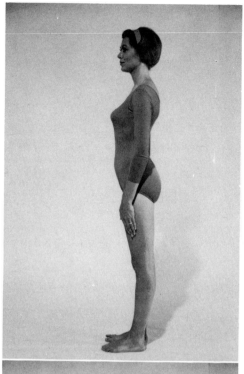

EXERCISE 14

The first illustration shows the starting position—an exaggerated low back curve with the pelvis tilted forward. The second illustration shows the exercise position, which is achieved by tightening the abdominal and gluteal muscles. The particular value of this exercise is the strengthening of muscles that help to maintain proper pelvic alignment for balanced posture. Again, the completed position should be sustained for ten counts.

Kinesiological Analysis:

▲ Factor most developed: Strength-tone.

▲ Muscles most involved: Rectus Abdominis, External Oblique, Internal Oblique, Transverse Abdominis, Gluteus Maximus.

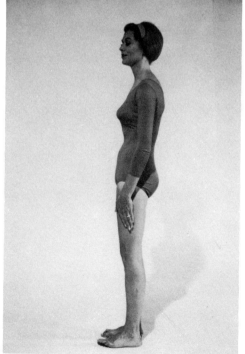

Two-Man
Isometric Exercises

EXERCISES 1 AND 2

These isometric sit-up exercises develop the abdominal muscles at two points within their range of motion. Since strength is most developed at the point of greatest resistance in the range of motion, these exercises impose resistance at two different points. Exercise 2 also contributes to the development of neck flexor strength. In important muscular areas such as the abdomen, it is recommended that resistance be applied at more than one point within the range to insure general strength development. Here again, is an application of the SAID principle: the musculature makes a specific, neuromuscular adaptation to the imposed demands. Note that in Exercise 1 the feet are held by the man providing the resistance whereas in Exercise 2 he stabilizes the legs with his forearm.

Kinesiological Analysis:

▲ Factor most developed: Strength-tone.

▲ Muscles most involved: Rectus Abdominis, External Oblique, Internal Oblique, Transversus Abdominis. Exercise 2 also involves the Sternocleidomastoideus.

EXERCISE 3

The purpose of this exercise is to develop the strength-tone of most of the posterior muscles. The person offering resistance allows the illustrated position to be assumed. At the height of the position, he offers sufficient resistance to force the individual out of position. The position should be held for ten counts.

Kinesiological Analysis:

▲ Factor most developed: Strength-tone.

▲ Muscles most involved: Erector Spinae, Rhomboids, Middle Trapezius, Gluteus Maximus, Semitendinosus, Semimembranosus, Biceps Femoris, Gastrocnemius.

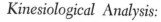

EXERCISE 4

The purpose of this exercise is to develop the strength-tone of the extensor muscles of the hips, knees, and ankles. To begin the exercise, the two men interlock their arms while standing back to back. The man exercising lifts his partner off the floor to the position shown. This is held for ten counts. As the individual increases tolerance for this exercise, progressively heavier persons should be lifted.

Kinesiological Analysis:

▲ Factor most developed: Strength-tone.

▲ Muscles most involved: Gluteus Maximus, Semitendinosus, Semimembranosus, Biceps Femoris, Rectus Femoris, Vastus Medialis, Vastus Intermedius, Vastus Lateralis, Gastrocnemius, Soleus.

EXERCISE 5

This exercise develops strength in the muscles of the rib cage that adduct the arms. The person kneeling forces the elbows downward while this effort is resisted by the second person. This should be sustained for ten counts.

Kinesiological Analysis:

▲ Factor most developed: Strength-tone.

▲ Muscles most involved: Biceps (short head), Coracobrachialis, Lower and Middle Pectoralis Major, Pectoralis Minor, Rhomboid, Latissimus Dorsi, Teres Major.

EXERCISE 6

This exercise is designed to develop strength-tone of the muscles that raise the arms sidewards. As the kneeling person exerts maximum effort upward, resistance is applied to prevent movement. This lasts for ten counts.

Kinesiological Analysis:

▲ Factor most developed: Strength-tone.

▲ Muscles most involved: Deltoid, Trapezius.

Exercise 7

This exercise develops the strength-tone of the muscles that raise the arm forward. Note the slightly flexed elbows of the kneeling man doing the exercise. This elbow position allows for greater exertion of force at the shoulder joint since the elbow joints are better stabilized. Maximum effort is exerted upward against the resistance for ten counts.

Kinesiological Analysis:

▲ Factor most developed: Strength-tone.

▲ Muscles most involved: Anterior Deltoid, Biceps, Serratus Anterior, Upper Pectoralis Major.

Exercise 8

This exercise develops strength in the muscles that pull the scapulae together and strengthens the back of the upper arm. To prevent excessive strain in the low back area, the knees of the person performing the exercise should be slightly bent. He attempts to force his elbows upward from the floor for ten counts, against the resistance provided by the second man.

Kinesiological Analysis:

▲ Factor most developed: Strength-tone.

▲ Muscles most involved: Rhomboid, Middle Trapezius, Posterior Deltoid, Long Head Triceps.

EXERCISE 9

The principal purpose of this exercise is to develop the muscles which flex the elbow. The standing person, who is doing the exercise, grasps the elbows of the kneeling man. With the back straight, he exerts maximum effort upward with his hands for ten counts.

Kinesiological Analysis:

▲ Factor most developed: Strength-tone.

▲ Muscles most involved: Biceps, Brachialis, and the Secondary Elbow Flexors of the Forearm.

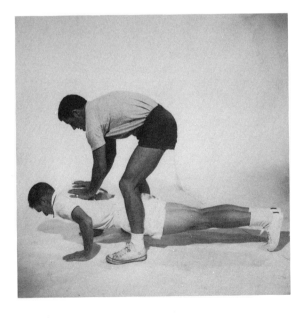

EXERCISE 10

This exercise develops the muscles of the chest and the back of the upper arms. Maximum effort should be exerted for ten counts as the movement is restricted by the individual offering resistance.

Kinesiological Analysis:

▲ Factor most developed: Strength-tone.

▲ Muscles most involved: Triceps, Pectoralis Major, Coracobrachialis, Short Head of Biceps, Anterior Deltoid.

EXERCISES 11 AND 12

These two exercises are designed to develop the extensor and flexor muscles of the neck, respectively. Each is a sustained isometric contraction for ten counts against the resistance provided by the second man.

Kinesiological Analysis:

▲ Factor most developed: Strength-tone.

▲ Muscles most involved: In Exercise 11: Upper portion of Erector Spinae Group. In Exercise 12: Sternocleidomastoideus.

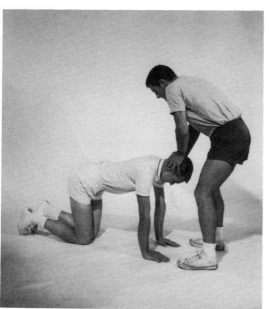

Door-Bar Series

The eight isometric door-bar exercises were designed to strengthen the major muscle groups of the body with maximum effectiveness and a minimum investment in time and equipment. The exercises comprise a basic program providing the essential minimum level of strength. This program, combined with flexibility exercises and endurance activities, satisfies the exercise requirements for most people, including those with sedentary occupations. Less than five minutes are required to complete all eight exercises, including the two changes of the door-bar position. These exercises may be combined with three minutes of two or three flexibility exercises and fifteen minutes of endurance or stamina-building activity such as rapid walking, rope skipping, swimming, bicycling, hiking, and jogging. The endurance-stamina exercises shown in this book would serve the same purpose. The recommended placement of the door-bar is based upon the requirements of a man five feet, ten inches tall with average bodily proportions.

EXERCISE 1

This exercise develops strength and tone of the abdominal muscles thereby developing a slimmer waist. In order to anchor the feet, the bar should be placed about four inches from the floor. With the knees bent so that the heels are about eight inches from the buttocks, the trunk is moved to, and held in, approximately a 45-degree angle for ten counts. If this position cannot be held for the count, the trunk should be held more erect to make such a sustained contraction possible. As the ability is developed to maintain the position with less stress, the 45-degree angle can then be approached. An effort should be made to flatten the abdominal wall while the position is held. For further intensification after the ten-count level has been reached, a weight, dependent upon the tolerance of the individual, may be held behind the head.

Kinesiological Analysis:

▲ Factor most developed: Strength-tone.

▲ Muscles most involved: Rectus Abdominis, External Oblique, Internal Oblique, Transverse Abdominis.

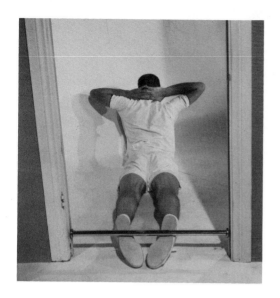

Exercise 2

This exercise involves the strength-tone development of most posterior muscles of the body. With the bar placed as it was in Exercise 1, the trunk is raised and sustained as high as possible for ten counts. This exercise may be intensified by holding a weight behind the head. As tolerance increases the amount of weight is increased.

Kinesiological Analysis:

▲ Factor most developed: Strength-tone.

▲ Muscles most involved: Erector Spinae, Posterior Deltoid, Rhomboids, Middle and Lower Trapezius, Gluteus Maximus, Semitendinosus, Semimembranosus, Biceps Femoris, Gastrocnemius.

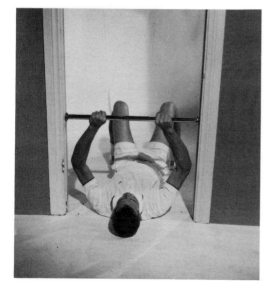

Exercise 3

This exercise develops the muscles of the chest and the back upper arm. Maximum effort should be exerted for ten counts. In this exercise the bar is moved to a position approximately 24 inches from the floor.

Kinesiological Analysis:

▲ Factor most developed: Strength-tone.

▲ Muscles most involved: Triceps, Pectoralis Major, Coracobrachialis, Short Head of Biceps, Anterior Deltoid.

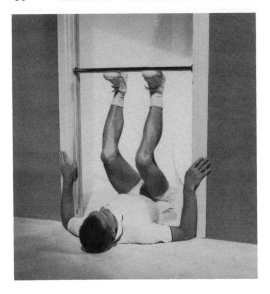

Exercise 4

This leg-extension exercise develops the strength-tone of the thighs, calves, and hip areas. With the bar placed approximately 36 inches from the floor, the front part of the sole of the foot is placed against the bar and maximum effort is exerted for ten counts. The feet should be separated about six inches, with legs parallel and the pelvis (sacrum) remaining on the floor. If the pelvis is raised, undue stress is placed on the lumbar spine which predisposes the area to injury.

Kinesiological Analysis:

▲ Factor most developed: Strength-tone.

▲ Muscles most involved: Gluteus Maximus, Semitendinosus, Semimembranosus, Biceps Femoris, Rectus Femoris, Vastus Medialis, Vastus Intermedius, Vastus Lateralis, Gastrocnemius, Soleus.

Exercise 5

With the bar directly overhead, 36 inches above the floor, a maximum effort is made to press upward. The back should remain straight. The effort is exerted for ten counts. This exercise develops the strength and tone of the muscles of the upper arm and shoulder area.

Kinesiological Analysis:

▲ Factor most developed: Strength-tone.

▲ Muscles most involved: Triceps, Deltoid, Trapezius, Serratus Anterior.

EXERCISE 6

With the bar at 36 inches, maximum effort should be made to pull downward from a sitting position for ten counts as in Exercise 5. The purpose of this exercise is to develop strength-tone of the muscles of the upper arm and the rib cage. If there is a tendency for the hips to leave the floor, strong contraction of the abdominal and hip flexor muscles should be made in an attempt to lift the feet as well.

Kinesiological Analysis:

▲ Factor most developed: Strength-tone.

▲ Muscles most involved: Biceps, Coracobrachialis, Lower and Middle of Pectoralis Major, Pectoralis Minor, Rhomboids, Latissimus Dorsi, Teres Major.

EXERCISE 7

This exercise, with the bar at 36 inches, is designed to develop strength and tone of the upper arm and shoulder area. While standing erect, a maximum effort should be made to pull the bar upward for ten counts.

Kinesiological Analysis:

▲ Factor most developed: Strength-tone.

▲ Muscles most involved: Biceps, Coracobrachialis, Upper and Middle portions of Pectoralis Major, Deltoid, Trapezius, Serratus Anterior.

EXERCISE 8

The purpose of this exercise is to develop the muscles of the front of the upper arm. Grasping the bar, which is placed about 36 inches high, with the palms upward, maximum effort is exerted for ten counts. An erect position of the back should be maintained.

Kinesiological Analysis:

▲ Factor most developed: Strength-tone.

▲ Muscles most involved: Biceps, Brachialis.

10

THE ISOTONIC
CONDITIONING EXERCISES

The type of exercise that has been most widely applied in the development of high level strength has been isotonic exercise. Isotonic exercises involve movement, in contrast to the isometric or no-movement exercises described in the last section. Although isometric exercise has been recommended for a most efficient gain in muscular strength for the amount of time invested, there are distinct advantages to be gained through isotonic exercise.

One of these advantages is the improvement in endurance-stamina which occurs at the same time as increased development of strength-tone. This improved stamina occurs because the body is forced to make circulatory adjustments in order to maintain muscle function during isotonic exercise. An increase in the capillary bed within the muscle may result from this type of exercise. This adjustment would be associated with improved stamina. In addition, this increased capillarization justifies isotonic exercise if an increase in the size of the muscle is desired. This type of exercise may also tend to thicken the muscle fibers which increases the bulk of the muscle. This may explain the noticeable gains in muscle bulk resulting from programs of isotonic exercise.

If the expenditure of time is not of particular importance, many find that isotonic exercise offers a more pleasant and satisfying approach to body development and maintenance than isometric exercise. More exhilaration results from moving the parts of the body against resistance rather than sustained tension against resistance without movement.

Another apparent advantage of isotonic exercises is the satisfaction of overcoming fixed amounts of resistance: it is possible to see what is accomplished. Effort does not result in observable work in isometric exercise, although maximum exertions are made. Still another advantage of isotonic exercise is that it functions through a full range of motion in a strength program and helps to promote or maintain flexibility.

These isotonic conditioning exercises were designed to progressively apply resistance using a minimum amount of equipment. It should be pointed out that the body, working against gravity, can serve as its own resistance; and in the design of these exercises this fact has been employed whenever possible. However, to sufficiently apply resistance in a developmental program, it sometimes becomes necessary to apply external resistance. For example, an individual with normal tolerance for exercise, flexing the elbow ten times would not impose sufficient demand for the development or maintenance of strength. To sufficiently impose demands on these muscles, it would be necessary to increase in some way the resistance against which they worked.

Although any external resistance that imposes demands would be effective in progressive conditioning, only bar bells are recommended in this series because of their adaptability and convenience. These weights have the advantage of being adjustable with known increments of resistance.

The direction of the pull of gravity, of course, remains constant regardless of the position of the body. Therefore, as the body changes position through exercise in relation to the direction of this pull, different muscles may be activated. Not only is the body position varied to increase resistance, but also external resistance is applied in the form of weight. This progression of activity and resistances in this series is in contrast to the exercises recommended in the isometric conditioning series, in which resistance is increased without altering body position or the equipment used.

This series of isotonic exercises was designed to avoid the use of elaborate equipment. Although no more equipment is required than that which is recommended in these exercises, this does not negate the use of other equipment. Spring devices, pulleys, counterbalance equipment, and other apparatus are effective in producing the some results.

By applying the SAID principle to isotonic strength development, it can be seen that increases will result only as muscles pull against increasingly heavy resistance. Since the ease, speed, and efficiency of strength development depends upon the number of repetitions, the exact amount of resistance, and other details, the following explanation is given.

Intensification of imposed demands. To develop strength, one must progressively overcome increased resistance. Light exercise, involving very little resistance, does not develop any appreciable amount of strength, no matter how often or how long it is done. For the development of strength-tone it is recommended that no more than twelve nor less than eight repetitions be performed for any one exercise. Experimentation with different levels of resistance is required to determine the precise amount of weight needed to impose demand within this range. Strength development will take place above and below these limits, but results are achieved more quickly when the resistance is graded rather precisely within the indicated range. Very heavy weight may cause muscle strain if progression to its use is not employed; very light weights reduce the efficiency of the process.

An ideal program with progressive weight resistance exercise is as follows: starting with a resistance that is great enough so that approximately eight repetitions can be accomplished, the exercise should be performed once during each work-out period. With each successive work-out, attempts should be made to increase the number of repetitions: additional repetitions should be made until one is able to perform approximately twelve. Resistance should then be increased so that approximately eight is again the maximum. This process of gradually increasing the resistance may be continued until the desired level of strength-tone has been achieved.

A few repetitions against a maximum resistance result in an adaptation which is mostly strength; performing many repetitions against a lighter resistance results principally in the development of endurance-stamina. In each case both characteristics are developed.

At the conclusion of each *exercise* one should be in a state of temporary, local, muscular fatigue. After each *work-out* he should be in a state of mild, general, muscular fatigue. Such fatigue is temporary, and quite different from the worn-out feeling that comes from emotional stress and overwork. Local fatigue should disappear after an hour. If it is found that fatigue persists following a night's sleep, the exercise program may be too heavy. After the first few work-outs, some residual muscular soreness and stiffness is normal. Soreness can be very bothersome but it disappears in a day or so because muscles soon adapt to the increased exercise.

Regularity. Widely separated, irregular exercise periods are undesirable. Demands should be imposed at least three times a week, and usually not more than five times a week. However, during the early stages of conditioning for strength development more frequent work-outs may be used. When the desired level of condition is approached, less frequent exercise periods are required.

Range of motion. When appropriate, each exercise should be carried through the extreme range of motion—to the limit of joint action. Each movement should be forced as far as possible, for flexibility is promoted in this way. If incomplete movements are habitually performed, adaptive shortening of the connective tissue may occur. For this reason general flexibility exercises are necessary to supplement isotonic conditioning exercise.

Breathing. During heavy work, there is a tendency to hold the breath. This action increases the air pressure in the chest cavity and has undesirable effects on blood pressure as well as inhibiting chest flexibility and expansion. Breathing should therefore be continuous when performing resistance exercise. In order to insure proper breathing, inhalation should take place during the hardest phase of the movement, while exhalation should accompany the easier phase. Holding the breath should be deliberately avoided. It must be understood, however, that breathing has nothing to do with the development of strength, but that it is employed only as a safety factor.

Maintenance of strength. Once desired levels of strength are reached through isotonic conditioning exercise, the principle of progression need no longer apply. That is, to maintain strength-tone, continually increasing demand level is not necessary. In addition, fewer exercise periods per week are required: a minimum of two periods is recommended.

Circuit Training

Circuit training is an effective use of isotonic conditioning exercise as a supplement to athletic conditioning programs. This modification of exercises recommended in this section, is an approach to conditioning developed by Morgan and Adamson in England. The approach differs somewhat from the isotonic conditioning series. In brief, a sequence of six to ten exercises that impose resistance are arbitrarily established. At the outset of the training program, an effort is made to achieve a maximum number of repetitions for each exercise. Once this has been done, this maximum number is reduced for each exercise by one third. It then becomes the object to complete circuits through all of the exercises in a progressively diminishing amount of time. Early in the training program, a circuit composed of ten exercises may be completed three times in approximately 30 minutes. This, of course, depends upon the number of exercises selected and the level of condition of the participants.

To impose increased demands, this procedure is altered periodically by increasing the number of repetitions and the amount of resistance when appropriate.

This type of intensification of demand appears to be the most efficient procedure for the simultaneous development of strength and endurance.

The following is an example of how a single exercise is employed in a circuit-training program. If an exercise for elbow flexion, such as biceps curls, is included, and 55 pounds of resistance has been arbitrarily established, and the person can perform 21 repetitions, the number of repetitions is decreased to 14 and the exercise is performed three times during the exercise period. That is, once during each circuit, 14 repetitions are performed of the biceps curl. To intensify this exercise in the circuit, the number of repetitions and the amount of resistance are increased periodically.

Any group of exercises may constitute the activities in a circuit, but consideration should be given for a selection of activities that would provide all-around development. A judicious selection of the exercises recommended in this isotonic conditioning series would provide the basis for an effective circuit-training program.

Circuit training has particular application to school programs and may be adapted to any existing facilities. Obviously, the exercises in this series may be supplemented by climbing ropes and other apparatus.

Isotonic Conditioning

Exercise 1

Basic to any conditioning program is the strengthening of the trunk muscle. In order to place the greatest stress on the abdominal muscles, the knees are flexed and the feet held down in some way. By placing the knees in this position, less of the action is accomplished by the muscles which flex the hip. The abdominal muscles are required to perform more of the work. It is recommended that the number of repetitions, with maximum effort, not exceed ten. That is, if more than twelve repetitions can be performed, more resistance should be applied. On the other hand, the resistance is too heavy if the movement cannot be done at least eight times. The amount of resistance may be varied either by altering the position of the body or by applying different amounts of externally applied resistance.

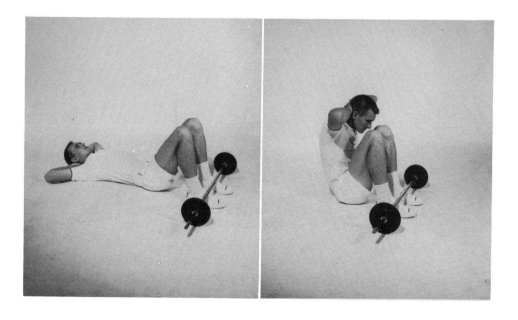

In this abdominal exercise, the trunk, head, and arms provide the resistance against which the abdominal muscles work. Individuals of low tolerance may not be able to perform the exercise with the arms in the position shown. If this is the case, the arms may be placed at the sides. To progress, the arms may be folded across the chest while the exercise is being performed. To further increase resistance, the fingers may be clasped behind the head and the elbows are held back as shown. The position of the body may be changed to provide increased resistance. This is done with a slant board. The resistance may be further intensified by holding a weight behind the head as illustrated.

Kinesiological Analysis:

▲ Factor most developed: Strength-tone.

▲ Muscles most involved: Rectus Abdominis, External Oblique, Internal Oblique, Transversus Abdominis.

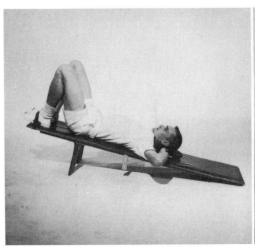

EXERCISE 2

To strengthen the posterior trunk, hips and thighs, the feet should be secured to provide the greatest stress on these muscles. The individual of low tolerance may hold his arms at the side while lying face down on the floor. A slant board may be used to increase difficulty. Resistance may be further intensified by moving the hands behind the head; still more, by adding weight. To offer resistance throughout a more complete range of motion, a bench or table may be used. Resistance should be increased so that no more than ten repetitions with maximum effort are possible.

Kinesiological Analysis:

▲ Factor most developed: Strength-tone.

▲ Muscles most involved: Erector Spinae, Gluteus Maximus, Biceps Femoris, Semitendinosus, Semimembranosus.

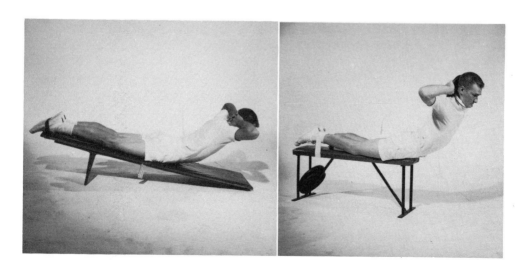

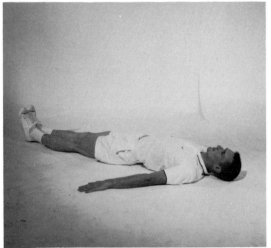

EXERCISE 3

This exercise is designed to strengthen most of the trunk muscles. The feet, held together, describe a large circle in the air. This slow, continuous motion, circling first to the right ten times and then to the left, involves lifting the hips as the feet circle overhead. Forceful action of the arms is required to execute this exercise. For individuals with lower tolerance, the knees should be bent to lessen the severity of the exercise.

Kinesiological Analysis:

▲ Factor most developed: Strength-tone.

▲ Muscles most involved: Rectus Abdominis, External Oblique, Internal Oblique, Transversus Abdominis, Erector Spinae, Triceps, Posterior Deltoid, Middle Trapezius, Rhomboids.

Exercise 4

This calf-strengthening exercise involves the use of a raised surface, approximately two inches high, to provide an increased range of motion for the ankle. As shown, this exercise may be done on one foot with the weight of the body providing resistance. Further intensification of this exercise may be accomplished by holding a weight across the back of the shoulders while on both feet. As increased tolerance develops, resistance should be increased so that no more than ten repetitions with maximum effort are possible.

Kinesiological Analysis:

▲ Factor most developed: Strength-tone.

▲ Muscles most involved: Gastrocnemius, Soleus.

Exercise 5

This exercise will increase the strength of the extensor muscles of the hip, knee and ankle. For those with low tolerance, a half knee-bend with both legs may be done. To increase the intensity, this same movement may be performed on one leg with the hand resting on some object for balance. Note that a wedge-shaped support is placed under the heel to provide more stability. As further intensification is required, a weight is held across the shoulders and a chair placed to the rear to prevent a deeper knee-bend. Resistance should be increased so that no more than ten repetitions with maximum effort are possible.

Kinesiological Analysis:

▲ Factor most developed: Strength-tone.

▲ Muscles most involved: Gluteus Maximus, Biceps Femoris, Semitendinosus, Semimembranosus, Gastrocnemius, Soleus.

EXERCISE 6

The push-up may be intensified in a number of ways to strengthen the muscles of the arms and chest. The individual with low tolerance in these muscles should begin by pushing up from a table or bench. The resistance may be intensified by having the hands level with the feet, and further intensified by elevating the feet above hand level. To provide additional resistance to these same muscles, a weight may be pressed upward while one lies on his back on a bench. Assistance may be required to place heavier weights in this position, as well as to be ready to remove the weight after ten repetitions against maximum resistance.

Kinesiological Analysis:

▲ Factor most developed: Strength-tone.

▲ Muscles most involved: Triceps, Pectoralis Major, Pectoralis Minor, Coracobrachialis, Short Head of Biceps, Anterior Deltoid, Serratus Anterior.

Exercise 7

The main purpose of this exercise is to strengthen the muscles that hold the shoulder blades in proper alignment. This exercise may be done in either the standing or lying positions shown. The trunk must be horizontal so that the resistance of gravity is in proper relationship. About ten repetitions should be accomplished against the most resistance made through the complete range of motion.

Kinesiological Analysis:

▲ Factor most developed: Strength-tone.

▲ Muscles most involved: Middle Trapezius, Rhomboids, Posterior Deltoid, Teres Major, Triceps.

Exercise 8

This exercise is to develop strength in arm and shoulder muscles. Although this exercise may be done standing, it is recommended that it be done in a sitting position in order to increase stability and avoid the possibility of excessive strain in the lumbar region of the back. Resistance should be increased so that no more than ten repetitions with maximum effort are possible.

Kinesiological Analysis:

▲ Factor most developed: Strength-tone.

▲ Muscles most involved: Trapezius, Serratus Anterior, Deltoid, Triceps.

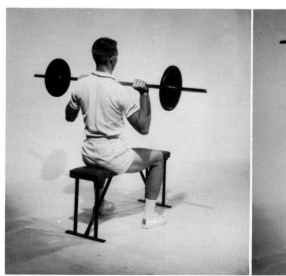 

EXERCISE 9

This exercise develops the muscles of the chest and arms. The particular value of this exercise is that it places stress on the latissimus dorsi muscles. These muscles pull the upper arm downward and can be strengthened in other ways, such as pull-ups, rope climbing, and the use of a pull-down apparatus. The exercise shown is, however, the most practical way of developing this area with the use of hand weights. This pull-over exercise is begun with the arms bent. The angle of the elbow does not change until the upper arm is nearly vertical, at which time the elbow is straightened. Caution should be taken to avoid excessive resistance when beginning this exercise in order to avoid injury to the shoulder joint. Resistance should be increased so that no more than about ten repetitions with maximum effort are possible.

Kinesiological Analysis:

▲ Factor most developed: Strength-tone.

▲ Muscles most involved: Latissimus Dorsi, Teres Major, Pectoralis Major, Pectoralis Minor, Rhomboids, Triceps, Coracobrachialis, Short Head of Biceps.

EXERCISE 10

This exercise strengthens the elbow and wrist flexors. This position with palms up, intensifies the action of the wrist flexors. If the bar were held with the palms down, greater stress would be placed on the extensors of the wrist. As far as strengthening the elbow flexors is concerned, there is little difference in these two hand positions. Care should be taken to avoid swinging the weight upward by swaying the body backward. Resistance should be increased so that no more than ten repetitions with maximum effort are possible.

Kinesiological Analysis:

▲ Factor most developed: Strength-tone.

▲ Muscles most involved: Biceps, Brachialis, Brachioradialis.

EXERCISE 11

This exercise is designed to place particular stress on the deltoid muscles. Resistance should be increased so that no more than ten repetitions with maximum effort are possible.

Kinesiological Analysis:

▲ Factor most developed: Strength-tone.

▲ Muscles most involved: Deltoid, Trapezius, Serratus Anterior, Biceps, Brachialis, Brachioradialis.

EXERCISE 12

This exercise develops strength in the muscles that elevate the shoulder girdle. Resistance should be increased so that no more than ten repetitions with maximum effort are possible.

Kinesiological Analysis:

▲ Factor most developed: Strength-tone.

▲ Muscles most involved: Upper Trapezius, Levator Scapulae.

EXERCISE 13

These movements against resistance strengthen the flexor and extensor muscles of the fingers and wrists. With the forearms resting on the thighs, the wrists are flexed and extended through a full range of motion. Ten repetitions against maximum resistance should be done with the palms up and with the palms down.

Kinesiological Analysis:

▲ Factor most developed: Strength-tone.

▲ Muscles most involved in *flexion at wrist*: Flexor Carpi Radialis, Flexor Carpi Ulnaris, Flexor Digitorum Sublimis, Flexor Digitorum Profundus.

▲ Muscles most involved in *extension at wrist*: Extensor Carpi Radialis Longus, Extensor Carpi Radialis Brevis, Extensor Carpi Ulnaris, Extensor Digitorum Communis.

EXERCISE 14

The purpose of this exercise is to develop the strength of the anterior neck muscles. Facing to the side with the head hanging over the end of a bench, the head is raised as high as possible while still turned. Resistance for this exercise may be increased by opposing the movement with the hand placed on the forehead. Resistance should be of such intensity that only ten repetitions can be performed to each side.

Kinesiological Analysis:

▲ Factor most developed: Strength-tone.

▲ Muscles most involved: Sternocleidomastoid.

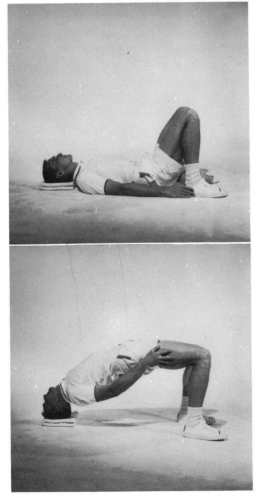

EXERCISE 15

This exercise develops the strength of the extensor muscles of the hip and back, with particular stress placed on the neck extensors. Since weight is borne by the head, a pad should be used to cushion the area. The amount of resistance imposed on the posterior neck muscles is dependent upon the position of the head. Bearing the weight on the back of the head is more strenuous than bearing it on top. Ten repetitions, moving from the lying to the arched position, are recommended. Changing the head position will intensify the exercise as tolerance increases.

Kinesiological Analysis:

▲ Factor most developed: Strength-tone.

▲ Muscles most involved: Erector Spinae, Gluteus Maximus.

11

FIGURE IMPROVEMENT
EXERCISES

Of particular concern to women is the contribution of exercise to figure improvement. Exercise is the only way to bring about better fitness *and* form. Exercise can help to develop a better looking body: it can slenderize and reshape, build-up and slim-down, and firm muscles that are lax and flabby. Through the improved function of postural muscles, better poise and carriage result. Almost everyone can benefit from a wisely selected program of exercise. Only through exercises that place sufficient demands on the body to develop stamina, suppleness, and muscle tone does figure improvement result. Often women tend to object to exercise because it is too strenuous. These objections generally arise through experiences with exercises that were beyond the tolerance of the individual. It must be realized that tolerance to perform exercise is progressively developed and that exercise must be selected to coincide with the tolerance of the individual. On the other hand, exercise that is not sufficiently taxing is of little value. Exercise too mild for the tolerance level of the individual will not produce the desired adaptations to imposed demands, and therefore cannot be expected to contribute to a figure improvement program. This is an application of the SAID principle described earlier. That is, specific adaptations result from imposed demands.

81

The exercises suggested in this figure improvement series are sequentially organized according to difficulty. Therefore, the successful performance of the more difficult exercises is an indication of increased tolerance.

Only by means of exercise that places sufficient demands on the body to improve, can body function or fitness be developed. And it is only through improved fitness that the figure can be improved. The person who says, "I am not interested in fitness, I'm interested in improving my figure," typifies the common misunderstanding about the role of exercise in figure improvement. A point difficult for women to understand is that there must be an exertion of near maximum effort to obtain observable results.

The exercises recommended in this series are primarily for strength or muscle tone. It is this factor which produces the firming and slenderizing effects most needed and wanted. To develop strength one particular factor must be observed. The resistance against which one forces muscles to work must be near maximum.

Another principle that should guide the development of a figure improvement program is regularity. Widely separated exercise periods or irregular periods are undesirable. At the outset of a figure improvement program daily exercise is recommended. After a period of time exercise should be done at least three times a week.

At the conclusion of each exercise there should be moderate, local fatigue in the muscles being used. At the conclusion of the exercise session the person should experience moderate, general fatigue. The intensity of the exercise may be determined by the amount of residual fatigue and muscle soreness. If general fatigue persists for over a period of approximately an hour following exercise, the session was probably too vigorous. The occurrence of bothersome muscle soreness beyond the second day following exercise is also an indication that the activity was too intense. On the other hand, mild muscle soreness is to be expected during the first week or two of an exercise program and should be no cause for alarm. Once the figure improvement program is underway, one might expect exhilaration rather than fatigue and soreness at the termination of the exercise series.

Generally, ten repetitions or ten counts of an exercise are advised. When it becomes easy to exceed this number, progression should be made to the next exercise in the sequence.

This figure improvement series has been designed to involve muscles in all body parts. Particularly emphasized are the exercises for the problem areas in figure improvement and maintenance: thighs, hips, waistline, bustline, and back of the upper arms. In addition to a lack of muscle tone, the principal problem with the figure is the lack of flexibility. Lack of flexibility or suppleness often prevents a balanced body carriage. This poor carriage tends to overemphasize figure faults.

The proper balanced alignment of the body is dependent upon the position of the pelvis. The relationship of posture or good body alignment to figure improvement cannot be overemphasized. Women who are unfit tend to lack sufficient muscle tone to maintain adequate body alignment. This results when these weakened muscles, lacking strength and tone, allow an increased low back curve which results in protruding abdomen and buttocks. Habitually remaining in this position results in adaptive shortening of the connective tissues in the low back area and the area in front of the hip joint. With such adaptive shortness, it becomes difficult to pull in the abdomen and buttocks and flatten the low back. This movement, involving the flattening of the low back curve and the tightening of abdominal and gluteal muscles, is known as a pelvic tilt. Even with sufficient strength, flexibility or suppleness is required in order to be able to perform this movement. For this reason the exercises recommended in the flexibility series become an important supplement to the exercises in the figure improvement series. This proper position of the pelvis promotes improved alignment of other body parts as well. The head and shoulder position is particularly influenced when the individual has sufficient tone and suppleness to assume and maintain a proper pelvic position.

Aside from weakness that results from lack of strength and tone, is another problem—the lack of stamina or staying power. A method of developing more stamina and delaying the onset of fatigue is to work at a rapid rate until breathless. Several of the exercises recommended in the figure improvement series can be used for this purpose. This might be accomplished by moving rapidly through the daily exercise session. Rest periods between exercises should be minimized. The continuity series of exercises are recommended for the person who desires greater stamina development. These exercises not only have the developmental features of the exercises recommended in the figure control series, but also are particularly suited to develop stamina because of their continual nature. An exercise program designed to promote endurance-stamina results in a mild state of fatigue that in turn provides natural relaxation.

Perhaps one of the most prevalent misconceptions regarding figure improvement is that fat deposits may be removed or displaced by pressures, massage, pinching, or pounding. There is no supporting evidence that these procedures result in any of the desired effects. If fat is to be lost in any part of the body, it is a result of the relationship between caloric intake and energy expended. A form of reproportioning through weight shift is possible, but this should not be confused with the effects of pounding, massage, and pinching. Fat is not broken down and reabsorbed in this way. It is, however, used as the body requires it for energy. In reproportioning, the effective procedure results from a greater caloric expenditure than intake and a development of muscular tissues where a build-up is desired. Reproportioning by this method is the only approach to slenderizing and recontouring the body. On the basis of what has been said, the idea that one may modify measurements without altering weight, is verified.

Although bodily proportions may sometimes drastically be altered through exercise, a realistic evaluation of one's figure potential must be made. Obviously, exercise is not a panacea. The contribution exercise can make to figure improvement is limited not only by desire and sustained effort but also by one's potentiality or capacity for improvement.

The use of exercise becomes increasingly important to counteract the inactivity that usually accompanies advancing age. Young women who exhibit the fitness and form of youth cannot expect to retain these characteristics unless they continue activity which imposes specific body demands. The less demand for physical activity there is in the normal course of living, the more important becomes a supplementary exercise program. In no other way is figure improvement possible.

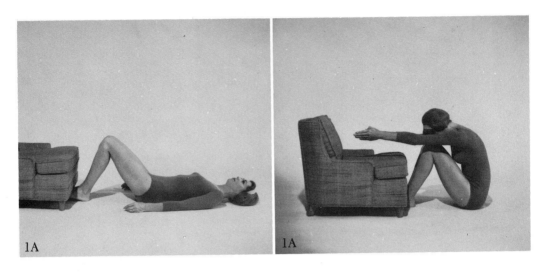

1A 1A

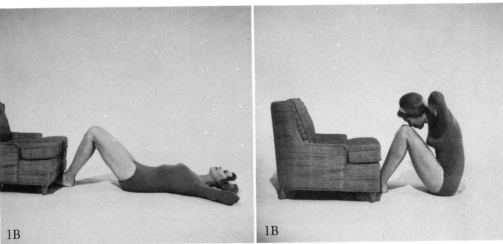

1B 1B

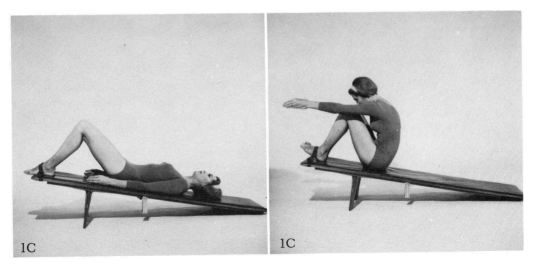

1C 1C

Figure Improvement
Exercises

EXERCISE 1

This is a waist-slimming and abdominal-flattening exercise which tones and strengthens the abdominal muscles. To place particular stress on the abdominal muscles, this exercise is done with the knees bent. In this position, the hip flexors are in a relatively slack position to minimize their function. This exercise may be done in several ways to provide a progression of resistance.

In this exercise the feet are anchored to provide better leverage for muscle action and to prevent the legs from lifting. Since this is predominantly an abdominal exercise, the objective is to bring the rib cage and the pelvis together by flexing the trunk toward the thighs. For maximum benefit, one should round the back while rising slowly: hold for two counts, then relax. Momentum or swing should be avoided so that greater demands are imposed on the abdominal muscles.

When 1A can be done more than ten times, 1B should be attempted and so on. If more demand is required after progressing through 1D, reference should be made to the abdominal exercises in the Isotonic Conditioning Series.

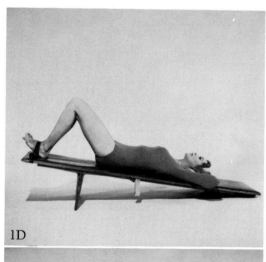

1D

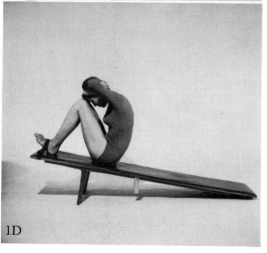

1D

Kinesiological Analysis:

▲ Factor most developed: Strength-tone.

▲ Muscles most involved: Rectus Abdominis, External Oblique, Internal Oblique, Transversus Abdominis.

EXERCISE 2

This exercise involves the anti-gravity muscles of the upper back. By strengthening these muscles an improved balanced posture may be maintained for a longer period. With the additional strength provided, fatigue is delayed. This improved ease with which better carriage may be maintained, results in better appearance. The muscles involved in this exercise, in terms of their potential, are generally the weakest in the body. For this reason marked gains can be expected.

In performing this exercise an effort should be made to lift the rib cage while pulling the shoulders back. After achieving ten repetitions of 2A, progress to 2B.

Kinesiological Analysis:

▲ Factor most developed: Strength-tone.

▲ Muscles most involved: Erector Spinae Group.

2A

2B

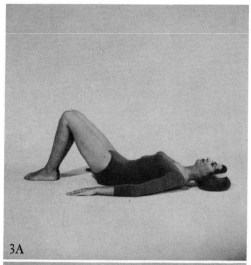

3A

EXERCISE 3

This exercise involves mainly the strengthening of the anti-gravity muscles of the lower back and contributes to firming the back of the upper arm if pressure is exerted downward with the hands.

To begin, the low back should be flattened against the floor to place the pelvis in the correct position for this exercise. Then the hips are slowly raised as high as possible from the floor. After holding for two counts, the hips are lowered to the starting position. When ten repetitions of 3A can be done easily, progress to 3B.

3A

Kinesiological Analysis:

▲ Factor most developed: Strength-tone.

▲ Muscles most involved: Erector Spinae Group, Gluteus Maximus, Biceps Femoris, Semitendinosus, Semimembranosus, Triceps.

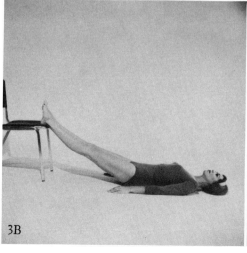

3B

3B

4A

EXERCISE 4

This exercise principally involves the diagonal muscles of the abdominal area and the low back, as well as contributing to the tone development of the back of the upper arm.

Exercise 4A and 4B have the same function, the difference evidenced in their progressive difficulty. As the ability to lower the hips alternately from side to side for more than ten times is developed, the legs should be straightened to increase the difficulty.

4A

Kinesiological Analysis:

▲ Factor most developed: Strength-tone.

▲ Muscles most involved: External Oblique, Internal Oblique, Transversus Abdominis, Rectus Abdominis, Erector Spinae, Middle Trapezius, Posterior Deltoid, Rhomboid, Triceps Brachialis.

4B

4B

5A

5A

5B

5B

EXERCISE 5

This progression of exercises strengthens and tones the thigh and hip area.

5A is done with the legs aligned with the body as balance is maintained with the arms. The uppermost part of leg, remaining straight, is raised as high as possible. After ten repetitions the exercise should be done lying on the other side, raising the opposite leg. When ten repetitions can be done easily, progress to 5B is indicated.

5B is done with the feet approximately 20 inches apart and legs straight. The hips are raised as high as possible and lowered ten times. When this exercise can be easily done ten times to each side, progression should be made to 5C.

5C involves raising both legs as high as possible while maintaining a straight line with the body, avoiding any flexion at the hips. When this exercise can be achieved with ease ten times to each side, progress should be made to 5D which involves the same muscles when repeated with each side.

Kinesiological Analysis:

▲ 5A: Factor most developed: Strength-tone.

▲ Muscles most involved: Right Gluteus Medius, Tensor Fasciae Latae.

▲ 5B: Factor most developed: Strength-tone.

▲ Muscles most involved: Left Gluteus Medius, Tensor Fasciae Latae, Right Adductor Magnus, Adductor Longus, Adductor Brevis, Gracilis, Pectineus.

5C

5D

▲ 5C: Factor most developed: Strength-tone.

▲ Muscles most involved: Right Gluteus Medius, Tensor Fasciae Latae, Left Adductor Magnus, Adductor Longus, Adductor Brevis, Gracilis, Pectineus.

▲ 5D: Factor most developed: Strength-tone.

▲ Muscles most involved: Left Gluteus Medius, Tensor Fasciae Latae, Right Adductor Magnus, Adductor Longus, Adductor Brevis, Gracilis, Pectineus.

Exercise 6

This exercise develops strength and tone in the back of the upper arm and the chest. In all cases, the hands are placed about a shoulder-width apart, the fingers aligned with the body.

Throughout these exercises the body should be held straight to avoid raising or sagging of the hips.

When 6A can be easily done ten times, progression should be made to 6B and so on.

6A

6A

6B   6B

6C

Kinesiological Analysis:

▲ Factor most developed: Strength-tone.

▲ Muscles most involved: Triceps, Pectoralis Major, Serratus Anterior.

EXERCISE 7

The purpose of this exercise is to increase the strength of the muscles that hold the shoulders back while the body is upright. Consequently, this assures better carriage and posture. This exercise may be done on the floor, but is best done on a more narrow surface such as the bench pictured. The weights should be raised as high as possible at each repetition. Resistance held in the hands should be light enough to permit ten repetitions of the movement. When more than ten repetitions can be done easily, the resistance should be increased. Although books are used in the illustrations, other forms of resistance, such as dumbbells, may be used.

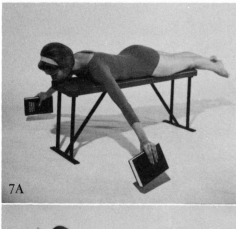

7A

7B

Kinesiological Analysis:

▲ Factor most developed: Strength-tone.

▲ Muscles most involved: Rhomboids, Middle Trapezius, Long Head of Triceps, Posterior Deltoid, Teres Minor, Teres Major, Infraspinatus.

EXERCISE 8

This exercise will strengthen and tone the muscles of the lower leg. Although no exercise can directly slim the ankle, an indirect function of this exercise is to help prevent swelling and puffiness in the tissues surrounding the ankle. Strengthening minimizes the excessive formation of tissue fluids and toning facilitates the return of blood through the veins. In addition to exercise, occasional elevation of the feet aids in fluid return.

Exercise 8A involves rising on the toes of both feet. If this can be accomplished easily ten times, progress should be made to exercise 8B. This same movement is intensified by elevating the body weight on one foot as balance is maintained by resting the hand on a chair as shown.

Kinesiological Analysis:

▲ Factor most developed: Strength-tone.

▲ Muscles most involved: Gastrocnemius, Soleus, Peroneus Longus, Peroneus Brevis, Posterior Tibialis, Flexor Hallicus Longus, Flexor Digitorum Longus.

EXERCISE 9

This exercise is primarily for strengthening and firming the thigh and buttocks areas.

Provided that there is sufficient strength to allow the performance of more than ten half knee-bends with both legs, as shown in 9A, progression should be made to 9B in which action in the same muscles of one leg is intensified by forcing that leg to perform the exercise. The chair is used to help maintain balance only: the hand should bear no weight.

Kinesiological Analysis:

▲ Factor most developed: Strength-tone.

▲ Muscles most involved: Vastus Medialis, Vastus Intermedius, Vastus Lateralis, Rectus Femoris, Biceps Femoris, Semimembranosus, Semitendinosus, Gluteus Maximus.

10A

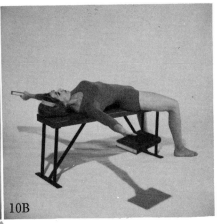

10B

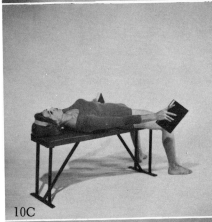

10C

10D

EXERCISE 10

The purpose of this exercise is to develop the strength-tone and bulk of the chest muscles, or the pectoral muscles. The use of exercise in improving the bustline is commonly misunderstood. It is known that exercise has no effect on the reshaping or contouring of the tissue of the breast. However, exercise can increase the size of the muscles that underlie the breasts.

Because of the variant functions of the pectoral muscles, three exercises are shown.

From each of the three starting positions, the arms are raised to the position shown in 10D. Each movement should be repeated ten times. If more than ten repetitions can be performed, the weight held in the hands should be increased so that no more than ten can be done. This exercise may be done on the floor but a bench is preferable because it allows the arms to be lowered through a complete range of motion, thus promoting flexibility.

Kinesiological Analysis:

▲ Factor most developed: Strength-tone.

▲ Muscles most involved: Pectoralis Major, Pectoralis Minor, Anterior Deltoid, Coracobrachialis, Short Head of Biceps.

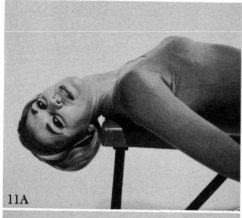

11A

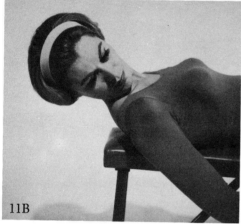

11B

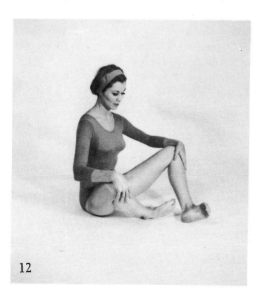

12

EXERCISE 11

The purpose of this exercise is to develop strength-tone of the front and side muscles of the neck. This exercise should be done with the head hanging and turned to the side as shown in 11A. The head should be raised ten times to the position shown in 11B; the exercise should be repeated with the head turned to the opposite side.

Kinesiological Analysis:

▲ Factor most developed: Strength-tone.

▲ Muscles most involved: Sternocleidomastoideus, platysma.

EXERCISE 12

Proper functioning of the foot plays an important role in postural alignment. If the longitudinal arch of the foot lacks strength and tone, compensatory adjustments are made which result in strain on other structures. Therefore, the strength of the feet is basic to proper carriage.

From a sitting position, the toes should be strongly curled under and inward ten times in succession. For those who have muscularly weak arches, it is suggested that the exercise be repeated intermittently throughout the day.

Kinesiological Analysis:

▲ Factor most developed: Strength-tone.

▲ Muscles most involved: Flexor Digitorum Longus, Flexor Digitorum Brevis, Flexor Hallicus Longus, Flexor Hallicus Brevis and other intrinsic muscles of the foot.

12

CONTINUITY
EXERCISES

This continuity series of exercises is for those who would enjoy a continuous movement experience while gaining muscle tone, flexibility, and stamina. These exercises are designed to place demands on all of the body areas in order to improve fitness and form. One advantage of these exercises is that they require no equipment and may be done in a relatively small space.

These movements resemble some elements of dance but they are not intended as such. They are based on a specific, musculature analysis of the involved body parts and should, therefore, be followed rather specifically if the intended benefits are to be achieved.

The person with low tolerance for exercise may experience some difficulty in performing these movements at first. However, an attempt should be made to perform the exercises as they are illustrated. Although an individual's performance may not be perfect, it is by making the effort to achieve the movement that tolerance is improved. Sufficient effort increases the tolerance for more exercise and ultimately provides adaptation and improved performance.

It is recommended that these exercises be done in the order they are presented. It is recommended also that each exercise be done during each exercise period: the exercises are designed to supplement each other. It is further recommended that, as the power to perform the exercises is increased, the number of times each exercise is performed also be increased. In this way these movements provide for the development of stamina as well as gains in muscle tone and flexibility.

Another method of increasing stamina by these exercises is to modify the rate of the performance. The rate of performance should be increased as the exercises are better managed. By functioning longer and more rapidly, functional limits are heightened. One way in which to sustain a continuous rate of performance is to accompany the exercise with appropriate music.

Through these continuity exercises, one may impose all the demands required for the development and maintenance of better fitness and form.

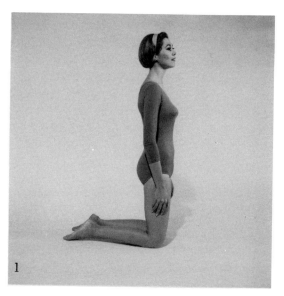

1

Continuity Series

EXERCISE 1

This exercise is a strength-tone and flexibility exercise which, if done at a sufficient rate and duration, also promotes endurance-stamina. The illustrations show positions within a continuous series of movements, that should be performed as one, over-all, flowing, rhythmic pattern without abrupt stops. The person begins by facing one direction and ends facing the opposite direction. The exercise is then repeated to the opposite side beginning with Illustration 3.

2

Movement ending in Illustration 2. As the body is caught by the hands and slowly lowered to the floor, the muscles of the back of the upper arm and chest are strengthened and toned. This is a push-up in reverse.

Kinesiological Analysis:

▲ Factor most developed: Strength-tone.

▲ Muscles most involved: Triceps, Pectoralis Major, Serratus Anterior.

Movement ending in Illustration 3. Moving to the position shown in Illustration 3 involves bending the left knee while raising the left hip and rotating the pelvis. This is followed by a push-off from the floor with the left arm raising the left shoulder and head.

Kinesiological Analysis:

▲ Factor most developed: Strength-tone: left hip, shoulder, arm.

▲ Muscles most involved: Strength-tone: Gluteus Maximus, Gluteus Medius, Triceps, Pectoralis Major, Serratus Anterior (left). Flexibility-suppleness: Rotators of the trunk, Pectoralis Major, Pectoralis Minor (right).

Movement ending in Illustration 4. This movement involves strength-tone in the muscles of the back of the upper arm and shoulder as well as the abdominal muscles which should be strongly contracted throughout the movement. In addition, this movement promotes the flexibility-suppleness of the upper back and neck.

Kinesiological Analysis:

▲ Factor most developed: Strength-tone: Triceps, Pectoralis Major, Serratus Anterior, Rectus Abdominis, External Oblique, Internal Oblique, Transversus Abdominis. Flexibility-suppleness: Rotators of the upper back and neck.

Movement ending in Illustration 5.
Without moving the feet or the right
hand, the hips are raised as far from
the floor as possible as the left hand
moves upward. This movement primarily develops the strength-tone of
the extensor muscles of the back and
the right leg, and the muscles of the
back of the right shoulder and arm.
Of particular value is the strong contraction in the adductors of the right
scapula. Especially important in moving to this position, is a strong contraction of the abdominal muscles to prevent an excessive low-back curvature.

Kinesiological Analysis:

▲ Factor most developed:
Strength-tone.

▲ Muscles most involved: Erector
Spinae , (at the hip) Gluteus Maximus, Semitendinosus, Semimembranosus, Biceps Femoris (right
shoulder), Triceps (long head), Posterior Deltoid, Teres Major, Middle
Trapezius, Rhomboid.

Movement ending in Illustration 6.
Except for flexion of the right knee as
the right foot is pulled into the position shown, the body position is unchanged. This position involves all of
the muscles described in the last movement, in addition to the flexors of
the right knee.

Kinesiological Analysis:

▲ Factor most developed:
Strength-tone.

▲ Muscles most involved: Erector
Spinae , (at the knee) Gluteus Maximus, Semitendinosus, Semimembranosus, Biceps Femoris (right
shoulder), Triceps (long head), Posterior Deltoid, Teres Major, Middle
Trapezius, Rhomboid.

Movement ending in Illustration 7. This movement involves a slow rock to the toes and forward to the knees, as the right hand slides forward to provide support. In this movement the abdominal muscles should remain contracted: this contraction helps to promote the flexibility of the hip flexor muscles during the movement.

Kinesiological Analysis:

▲ Factor most developed: Strength-tone.

▲ Muscles most involved: Rectus Abdominis, External Oblique, Internal Oblique, Transversus Abdominis, Rectus Femoris, Vastus Medialis, Vastus Intermedius, Vastus Lateralis.

Movement ending in Illustration 8. This is a return to the kneeling position facing the other direction.

7

8

Exercise 2

This exercise is designed primarily to develop strength-tone. If done rapidly and long enough, these movements contribute to the development of endurance-stamina. This exercise should be repeated to the opposite side.

Movement ending in Illustration 2. As a strong contraction is maintained with the abdominal muscles and those of the front thighs, the body is allowed to slowly move backward until the right hand contacts the floor.

Kinesiological Analysis:

▲ Factor most developed: Strength-tone.

▲ Muscles most involved: Rectus Abdominis, External Oblique, Internal Oblique, Transversus Abdominis, Rectus Femoris, Vastus Medialis, Vastus Intermedius, Vastus Lateralis.

1

2

Movement ending in Illustration 3. When the right hand, bearing part of the body weight, contacts the floor it slides along the floor allowing the body to be lowered. At the same time the body is rolled to the right. This movement involves the muscles of the rib cage and right shoulder. Abdominal contraction should be maintained throughout the movement.

Kinesiological Analysis:

▲ Factor most developed: Strength-tone.

▲ Muscles most involved: Pectoralis Major, Pectoralis Minor, Coracobrachialis, Short Head of Biceps, Long Head of Triceps, Latissimus Dorsi.

Movement ending in Illustration 4. Before the hips are lifted, the right arm is moved to a position along the side with the back of the hand against the floor. The left leg maintains the body balance in this position while the major effort is made with the muscles along the right side of the body. This movement primarily develops the strength-tone of the area of the right hip.

Kinesiological Analysis:

▲ Factor most developed: Strength-tone.

▲ Muscles most involved: Gluteus Medius, Tensor Fasciae Latae, Rectus Abdominis, External Oblique, Internal Oblique, Transversus Abdominis.

5

6

7

Movement ending in Illustration 5. This movement involves lowering the hips to the floor while rolling further to the right until the face-down position is assumed.

Movement ending in Illustration 6. The feet lead the movement by rolling to the left as the trunk is pushed up with the arms.

Kinesiological Analysis:

▲ Factor most developed: Strength-tone.

▲ Muscles most involved: Triceps, Pectoralis Major, Serratus Anterior, Anterior Deltoid.

Movement ending in Illustration 7. This movement involves rolling the pelvis to a sitting position by contracting the abdominal muscles and pressing against the floor with the left hand.

Kinesiological Analysis:

▲ Factor most developed: Strength-tone.

▲ Muscles most involved: Rectus Abdominis, External Oblique, Internal Oblique, Transversus Abdominis, Triceps.

Movement leading to the return to the starting kneel position involves a brisk push with the left hand against the floor while the pelvis is shifted over the feet before lifting the hips.

Kinesiological Analysis:

▲ Factors most developed: Strength-tone.

▲ Muscles most involved: Triceps, Gluteus Maximus, Rectus Femoris, Vastus Medialis, Vastus Intermedius, Vastus Lateralis.

Exercise 3

This exercise is designed to develop tone and suppleness in specific regions of the body as it is done smoothly and continuously at a moderate rate.

1

2

Movement ending in Illustration 2. From the starting position, balancing on the left foot, the right leg swings to the rear together with a backward movement of the arms and head.

Kinesiological Analysis:

▲ Factor most developed: Strength-tone: Endurance-stamina.

▲ Muscles most involved: Strengthened: Rhomboids, Middle Trapezius, Erector Spinae, Gluteus Maximus, Biceps Femoris; Semitendinosus, Semimembranosus. Stretched: Pectoralis Major, Iliopsoas.

Movement ending in Illustration 3. This position is reached by allowing the left knee and hip to flex slowly while the right foot is returned to the floor.

Kinesiological Analysis:

▲ Factor most developed: Strength-tone.

▲ Muscles most involved: Gluteus Maximus, Rectus Femoris, Vastus Medialis, Vastus Intermedius, Vastus Lateralis.

Movement ending in Illustration 4. This is a continuation of the last movement. The knee and hip are flexed to lower the body further so that the left hip and knee extensors are strengthened as the right hip flexors are stretched. This movement is one of the few which can sufficiently stretch the hip flexors.

Kinesiological Analysis:

▲ Factor most developed: Strength-tone;   Flexibility-suppleness.

▲ Muscles most involved: Strengthened: Gluteus Maximus, Biceps Femoris, Semitendinosus, Semimembranosus, Rectus Femoris, Vastus Intermedius, Vastus Medialis, Vastus Lateralis.
Stretched: Iliopsoas.

5

6

7

Movement ending in Illustrations 5 and 6. With the body moved slightly upward, a slow twist of the spine is first made to the left and then to the right. These twisting movements should be continued through a full range of motion and should be momentarily sustained at the extreme limit of the range.

Kinesiological Analysis:

▲ Factor most developed: Flexibility-suppleness.

▲ Muscle groups most involved: Spinal Rotators, Oblique Abdominals.

Movement ending in Illustration 7. The left knee and hip are strongly extended, pushing the body backward. While the left foot is being drawn to the rear, the trunk is bent forward, slowly stretching the posterior muscles of the thighs and back.

Kinesiological Analysis:

▲ Factor most developed: Flexibility-suppleness.

▲ Muscles most involved: Erector Spinae, Gluteus Maximus, Biceps Femoris, Semitendinosus, Semimembranosus.

Movement ending in Illustration 8. This illustration shows the back held straight as the individual returns to an upright position.

Kinesiological Analysis:

▲ Factor most developed: Strength-tone.

▲ Muscles most involved: Erector Spinae, Gluteus Maximus, Biceps Femoris, Semitendinosus, Semimembranosus.

Illustration 9: Self-explanatory.

Movement ending in Illustration 10. This is the beginning of the continuity exercise done to the opposite side.

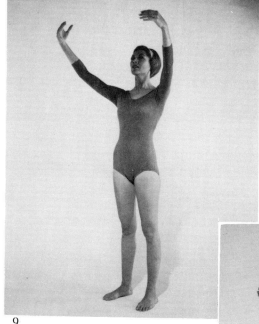

8

9

10

EXERCISE 4

Movement ending in Illustration 1. This continuity exercise is begun by rising on the toes to strengthen and tone the calf muscles. The arms are simultaneously swung upward.

Kinesiological Analysis:

▲ Factor most developed: Strength-tone.

▲ Muscles most involved: Gastrocnemius, Soleus.

Movement ending in Illustration 2. From the upright starting position, the knees are allowed to slowly flex, strengthening the muscles in front of the thigh and in back of the hip. The arms are moved into position ready to support the body for the backward, rolling movement to be made next.

Kinesiological Analysis:

▲ Factor most developed: Strength-tone.

▲ Muscles most involved: Gluteus Maximus, Rectus Femoris, Vastus Medialis, Vastus Intermedius, Vastus Lateralis.

Movement ending in Illustration 3. This illustrates the continuation of the backward rolling motion. After the hands have broken the fall, the arms are moved sidewards as the legs are straightened upward.

Movement ending in Illustration 4. The arms are moved to a position at which pressure can be exerted downward to assure continued rolling motion. With the legs straight, the abdominal muscles are strongly contracted to continue the movement.

Kinesiological Analysis:

▲ Factor most developed: Strength-tone;   Flexibility-suppleness.

▲ Muscles most involved: Strengthened: Triceps, Rhomboids, Middle and Upper Trapezius, Rectus Abdominis, External Oblique, Internal Oblique, Transversus Abdominis. Stretched: Erector Spinae.

Movement ending in Illustration 5. Rolling back from the position in which the legs were over the head, the abdominal muscles are contracted in order to stabilize the pelvis. In this way the legs may be held up and apart in a "V-sit" position. Just before this position is reached, the hands are lifted from the floor.

Kinesiological Analysis:

▲ Factor most developed: Strength-tone.

▲ Muscles most involved: Rectus Abdominis, Vastus Medialis, Vastus Intermedius, Vastus Lateralis, Iliopsoas, Adductor Magnus, Adductor Longus, Adductor Brevis, Gracilis.

Movement ending in Illustration 6. As the left knee is flexed and moved to the floor, the left hand is simultaneously placed on the floor. The body is then turned to the left and raised with the left arm and leg. This movement is designed to strengthen and tone the muscles of the side of the hips and thighs.

Kinesiological Analysis:

▲ Factor most developed: Strength-tone.
▲ Muscles most involved: Gluteus Maximus, Gluteus Medius, Triceps.

Movement ending in Illustration 7. This slow return to the "V-sit" involves the same muscles used in the movement from the "V-sit" to the side-facing position on the knee and hand just described. From this "V-sit" position, the side-facing position is assumed on the other side. Then a return is made to the "V-sit" and the legs are brought together to prepare for another backward rolling movement.

9

Movement ending in Illustration 9. A return to the starting position is made by rolling forward, flexing the knees, and assuming the upright position shown at the beginning of this continuity exercise. This last movement develops the strength-tone of the muscles of the back of the hip and the front of the thigh.

Kinesiological Analysis:

▲ Factor most developed: Strength-tone.

▲ Muscles most involved: Gluteus Maximus, Rectus Femoris, Vastus Medialis, Vastus Intermedius, Vastus Lateralis.